A LIFE FULL OF
GLITTER

Mango Publishing Group
2850 Douglas Road, 3rd Floor
Coral Gables, FL 33134 U.S.A.
info@mango.bz

For special orders, quantity sales, course adoptions and corporate sales, please email the publisher at sales@mango.bz. For trade and wholesale sales, please contact Ingram Publisher Services at: customer.service@ingramcontent.com or +1.800.509.4887.

A Life Full of Glitter: A Guide to Positive Thinking, Self-Acceptance, and Finding Your Sparkle in a (Sometimes) Negative World

Library of Congress Cataloging
ISBN: (print) 978-1-63353-814-6 (ebook) 978-1-63353-815-3
Library of Congress Control Number: 2018952300
BISAC category code: SEL023000 SELF-HELP / Personal Growth / Self-Esteem

Printed in the United States of America

A LIFE FULL OF
GLITTER

A Guide to Positive Thinking,
Self-Acceptance, and Finding Your Sparkle
in a (Sometimes) Negative World

ANNA O'BRIEN
Creator of Glitter + Lazers

mango

CORAL GABLES

This is dedicated to Mirah and Garrett.
May you be the future the world needs.

CONTENTS

INTRODUCTION

I can't believe I did it. I actually wrote a book. There are
moments in our lives when things seem overwhelming and
impossible. Creating this book was one of those times. I
felt stressed out, nervous, insecure, and fearful. *Would my
words be good enough*?

I had every reason to be nervous. While writing this book, I
shared more of my life, opinions, and challenges than ever
before. There were days I spent hours crying as I wrote out
painful memories and lessons from my past, and others
when I was reminded just how much we can all grow and
change. These pages are filled with love and experience.
That's the best thing I can offer to a world in need of
greater understanding.

In each chapter you'll find a mix of personal stories,
scientific research to increase our understanding on
different topics, and active steps you can take to better
your own life. This formula is important to me. I believe the
more we understand how our brains and bodies work, the
more connected to them we become. That connection is
powerful and is fundamental to better understanding our
needs and emotions in the present.

As I wrote each chapter, I re-learned lessons, grew stronger
in my commitment to changes I'd made in my past, and
uncovered the scientific explanation for things that always
made sense to me but I could never fully explain. This book
isn't just a guide to thinking more positively, but rather a

collection of the tools that I have used to develop into the strong, fearless, and positive person I am today—and how you can too. Writing this book helped me grow. I hope reading it will do the same for you.

CHAPTER 1

THE BENEFITS OF A MORE POSITIVE LIFE

"We are all in the gutter, but some of us are looking at the stars."

—**Oscar Wilde,** *Lady Windermere's Fan*

I used to think of positivity as so lame. I can't think of a better way to describe it—"so lame" suits the way my teenage brain processed it all at the time. Do you remember those men in fresh pressed suits on big stages with tiny headband microphones, selling us the power of positivity on late night infomercials? They'd wave their hands around until they were drenched in sweat from preaching the power of optimism. They looked so mature and chiseled (albeit caked in perspiration)—totally un-relatable to a teenage girl who felt misunderstood. How could a real-life aged-Ken-doll fathom the struggles of a chubby, geeky girl with acne, bullies, and a crush on every boy? I was convinced it was all a sham. I'd shut off the TV, envious that Ken got to live his perfect life, complete with a custom-made Italian suit and fancy mini-microphone, while I still had to make a diorama explaining the plot of *To Kill a Mockingbird* out of toothpicks and crushed dreams.

I should note that when I was thirteen, I was angry and deeply sad. My home life was challenging, I definitely didn't have the media-driven "cool teenager" body, and I was awkward. I was really awkward. Eventually that sadness spilled out into my life through anger. I cussed, I fought and I got in too much trouble. I was so unruly that I was sent to a special school for wayward children. Perhaps this sounds like the plot of a well-orchestrated children's novel. It's not. People simply began to lose faith in me and as a result, I began to lose faith in myself.

On the outside, I became the neighborhood child that parents didn't want their kids to play with. On the inside, I was a mixed bag of negative emotions. I felt lonely, angry at the world, envious of those with simpler lives, and confused as to who I was. I was desperate to turn my life around, but given the circumstances it all seemed overwhelming and hopeless.

I remember very clearly sitting in this classroom of unruly children pondering my future. To the left a teacher was literally tackling a student who'd begun a violent outburst. To the right, another student was slowly punching the front of their forehead over and over; sometimes the person we bully most is ourselves. In this terrible moment, I realized something had to change. Maybe it was some sort of divine intervention or, maybe just maybe, I was sick and tired of the person I was. I couldn't change the circumstances around me, so I would have to be the one to change. If I didn't, my life would be a complete waste. It was then that my story began to evolve.

Maybe that's how you feel right now. Maybe that's why you're reading this book, because you too realize something in your life has to change, but you're not sure what or how to do it. It's a process. It would take me a few years to get my footing and to fully integrate positivity into my life. I want to start this book off with honesty. The change you want does not happen overnight, even though I would love for that to be the case. Miracles are not worked in an hour of light reading. It didn't happen that way for me, and I am pretty confident that it doesn't happen that way for most people. You have to put in the work to change.

By the time I got to college, my life was unrecognizable from who I previously was. I entered university on an exception—my grades had been too poor during my rebellious days to go to most schools. However, my new found positivity was a force to be reckoned with. I found an exceptions committee, prepared my case, and found my way into a good school anyway. I went from a C-minus student in high school to an A student in college. Once an awkward loner, I became a social butterfly.

I attribute the majority of my growth in those years to positivity. I was committed to the belief that things would get better, I would get better, and as a result the world would get better. That belief in a better life molded me into the lady boss I am today. I fought to recognize and appreciate many more things in my daily life. I became more present in my reality, and as result I saw and believed I was worthy of so many more opportunities. I developed a deep sense of gratitude, so when bad things happened I was able to acknowledge them as a temporary part of the cycle.

When I tell you that optimism can change your life, I tell you as a person who personally experienced it. I am who I am because I chose to live a more positive life. It may seem impossible at first, but if you invest the time, you will see a whole new world of possibilities open up to you. It will give you the ability to recognize and take advantage of all the amazing things in your life you may be overlooking, help you find the power to overcome hardship more quickly, and it will become your rock-solid foundation for a happier life.

I can see you sitting there, reading my story and making me out to be an exception to the rule. I got lucky. I was an anomaly. I can't blame you; old me would have done the exact same thing. Maybe I come across like a modern version of that dapper man and his tiny headset. However, I want to stress to you that my growth is not unique. I've rounded up a bevy of research that helps to support that my story can become your story as well. You too can choose to live and receive all the benefits of living life on the sunny side. In fact, it is the scientifically expected outcome of a life lived with zeal. Studies have shown that people that incorporate positivity into their lifestyle better cope with stress, have stronger immune systems, better overall health, and are more resilient when crises do happen. Optimists are also statistically more likely to notice opportunities in their social and work lives.

POSITIVE THINKERS COPE BETTER WITH STRESS

Have you ever been at work or school and gotten a message that you needed to meet with a boss or teacher and then worried the entire day about what the meeting could be about? Maybe you failed. Maybe you've done some terrible awful thing you somehow managed to forget. Maybe a terrible rumor about you has spread like wildfire and you're going to have defend yourself. So you spend the next several hours until the meeting running over every possible negative reason for the meeting. Your palms are sweaty. Your mind is cloudy. You are engulfed in your own anxiety. Then the big sit-down finally rolls around and you find out you just forgot to submit some paperwork or some other mundane thing. The stress you felt all day was unnecessary, and as a result a huge amount of your precious emotional energy was wasted. Most of our day-to-day stress—just like in this example—is self-created.

According to research, stress itself doesn't exist in an event, but rather in our perception of an event.[1] In simple terms, it means that no matter what happens in life, you have the ability to be in the emotional driver's seat. Pessimists often approach commonplace life situations with the expectation that they've done something wrong. In the previous example, many of us frequently assume that the only reason a boss or teacher might ever speak to us is because we've done something wrong. This type of thinking not only creates additional stress, but closes us off from opportunities and friendships, and it can affect our ability to manage stress in the long run. Optimists, on the other hand, do not adopt a sentiment regarding a given situation until all the facts needed to fairly assess it are available. It's not that the optimist is assuming that something amazing is going to happen at the meeting. They're not sitting anxiously, counting down the hours until their office pow-wow so they can get some super fun prize. They're simply not assuming anything at all.

If the event is negative, the positive individual benefits from the fact they haven't been mulling over every possibility and creating a million-and-one negative scenarios in their head. This makes them more prepared to manage the real results of the situation, less likely to overreact as result of pent-up emotion, and generally more able to resolve any issues that they are faced with. In this way, positive people are problem-solvers and rely on coping skills versus venting or fixating on the issue at hand.[2]

I should share that this has been one of the hardest things I've ever had to learn. In the early stages of my career, when a problem would arise, I would have to tell no less than every single person in my office, the doorman, and several strangers I wrestled into conversation on the street before I could put the issue to rest. Sometimes even that wasn't enough. I'd find myself like a car caught in quicksand—spinning my wheels with all this excess emotion, but getting nowhere. Venting our issues, while seemingly harmless and perhaps even possibly therapeutic, can cause us to fixate on the negative aspects of an incident rather than invest our energy in resolving its challenges.

I remember talking with my boss about an issue I was, once again, ruminating on. He stopped me dead in my tracks, looked me square in the eye, and said: "Is talking about this actually making anything better for you?" It wasn't. I apologized, and he grinned. He stood up from his desk, spread his arms wide, leaned back, and started to sing. "Let it go... Let it *go-oh-oh-oh*." To this day, whenever I find myself obsessing over something that does not deserve my emotional energy, I stand up, spread my arms wide, and sing that song. It never fails to turn my mood around. It took a Disney princess for me to break one of my most resilient pessimistic habits.

Let this story help you to remember that you have a choice as to where you invest your energy. Perhaps when things go awry, you too can be like Elsa, the famous ice princess from Frozen—let it go and remember that most of the stress in your day-to-day life can be avoided or even reduced by keeping an upbeat attitude. Research has found that optimists not only create less stressful situations, but also experience less overall stress than non-optimists.[3] As I grow into my own optimism, I find I tend to let go of negative events more quickly. This keeps stressful situations from piling up and becoming overwhelming.

I've also been able to build better support systems, because I've stopped assuming the worst about every situation I enter. When stressful situations arise, I'm able to reach out to my friends and rely on them to help me through. When you start to see the good in things, you have better relationships and less stress, and you can let go of some of your unnecessary baggage. I think we can all agree that the world could use a few more people who leave their baggage at home.

POSITIVE THINKING IS GOOD FOR YOUR HEALTH

I remember one morning in my childhood when I desperately wanted to avoid going to school. I had a brand new Sega Genesis video game system, and school was an obstacle to my short-term happiness. I wanted to be sick so badly that every day I would dramatically cough whenever my parents were around. I would complain about how my throat hurt and then dramatically fall backward onto the floral cushions of our living-room sofa. I was in agony, or so I wanted my parents to think.

Eventually my mother was annoyed by my theatrics and informed me that we would be going to the doctor for a professional opinion. She had called my bluff. I was done for. She was going to find out I was lying and then punish me. Nothing is scarier than a mother who proves you wrong. I remember I was so fearful of impending mom-wrath that I rummaged through our freezer to find a popsicle, downed it, and literally scraped the back of my throat with the popsicle stick in a desperate attempt to create the appearance of an illness that I 100 percent did not have.

As we sat in the doctor's waiting room, I remember the tension being unbearable. It was one thing to be at the doctor's (the worst place ever!), but being caught doing the worst thing ever (lying!) at the worst place ever?! I was stress-ball-wrapped in worry, not to mention being dusted with a whole lot of regret. By the time we actually were called in to be seen, I was sweating and unpredictably tired. The doctor swabbed my throat and I awaited my inevitable disastrous fate.

To my surprise, the test came back positive. I had strep. I fervently believe when I look back on that scenario that I worried myself into that sickness. I told a lie, got in too deep, and the sheer fear of being found out broke down my immune system. Now that I've learned a bit about how negative thinking can destroy the effectiveness of our immune system, I realize that this isn't that far-fetched an idea to believe.

Some of the top medical research centers in the US are actively researching how negativity affects our overall health. The Mayo Clinic has found that negative thinking can increase your need for medical care, raise your chances of heart disease, and even lower your ability to fight serious illnesses.[4] To illustrate just how powerfully positive thinking and behaviors can alter your health, here are three studies on how positivity affects health that I find mind-blowing:

As part of a study at the University of Missouri, students did positive journaling once a day, three times a week. At the end of three months, they reported better moods and had fewer health center visits than those who did not journal.[5]

Researchers at John Hopkins University spent twenty-five years keeping track of a group of people with family histories of heart disease. Over that period, participants who lived a positive lifestyle were one-third less likely to have a heart attack or other cardiovascular event.[6]

A study of post-operative breast cancer patients conducted by Indiana University found that those who lived a positive lifestyle saw less of a dip in their levels of natural killer cells, which is a type of white blood cell that can kill tumor cells or cells infected with a virus. These cells are vital to the long-term healing process, meaning that a positive lifestyle left post-op patients with a more robust immune system.[7]

These are just a small sample of the hundreds of articles that I came across that link a cheerful disposition with better long-term health. I learned that optimists experience less pain,[8 9 10 11] have improved heart function,[12] live longer,[13] and have stronger immune systems. I should note that being a positive person doesn't mean you should obsess over living a perfect healthy lifestyle. In fact, simply choosing to live your life on the sunny side of the street will naturally make you tend toward making healthier life choices.[14]

One major change in my day-to-day life, versus back when I was an angry "Negative Nancy," is that I *smile* more. Usually, when my eyes catch a stranger on the street, I flash them a grin. I started doing this because I decided that I wanted to treat the world the way I hoped to eventually be treated. Back then, not many people looked at me and smiled; I was determined to change that.

Now, I didn't adopt this habit for the purpose of improving my overall physical health, but rather as an attempt for me to try build a better connection with the people around me and, as a result, with the world. However, I have learned that even small positive gestures, like my goofy grin, can make significant impacts on your overall health. A study by the University of Kansas found that smiling—even if it's a fake, totally forced smile—reduces your heart rate and blood pressure during stressful situations.[15] This is a great example of how resolving to act in a more positive fashion can turn out to be a physically healthy choice, without your even knowing it!

Simple Ways to Boost Your Health with Positivity

1. Keep a daily journal of positive things happening in your life.

2. Take a short walk around your neighborhood and smile at the people you pass.

3. Every time you find yourself in front of a mirror, say something kind to yourself.

4. Call someone you love and tell them how important they are to you.

POSITIVITY MAKES YOU MORE RESILIENT

When I was a teenager, a book series called *Chicken Soup for the Soul* became overwhelming popular. In this series, people could read heartfelt stories of people who overcame struggles in inspiring and tear-jerking ways. You could read about a three-legged, blind dog that saved children from a burning building, a homeless man who became a billionaire by selling tube-tops out of the trunk of his rundown car, or a barren woman who adopted children who then went on to become professional foosball players. *Psych!* I made those stories up, but these are the kind of mind-blowing, heroic stories you can find in a whole plethora of inspirational books which follow the *Chicken Soup* model.

The individuals in these beloved stories experienced the same traumas we experience every day, but managed to bounce back even better than before. Many of us crumble when we experience a negative event. Not in these books. We love reading stories of shocking heroism: "Most dogs would run *away* from the blazing fire! But not you, Rocky the pup with no eyes and all the heart—you just kept going! Wow. Just, *wow*." We loved these stories, because they were inspirational; somehow, these people (and animals) beat the odds. We saw their strength at the forefront of their resilience, but if we had only looked a little closer we might have seen something else. Our paperback "chicken soup heroes" were, more often than not, positive people.

Many believe resilience is a personality trait: you're either born with it or you're not. However, I believe that it's actually a dynamic learning process, and the research backs me up.[16] The more optimistic you became about yourself and your life, the more you are able to not sweat the small stuff and the better you'll make it through the big, scary, heart-pounding stuff. You must learn to logically analyze situations in moments of stress and place whatever crazy incident you're experiencing in the context of the bigger picture. This will help keep you focused and allows you to understand the actual importance of the whole episode versus the catastrophic story that unmitigated shock automatically tells you is going on.

Plus, even in life's crummiest, saddest, and most devastating moments, there is usually a silver lining. Drawing on skills such as problem-solving and self-assessment, you have the opportunity to learn and grow from each negative event instead of focusing on how utterly unbearable the situation is making your life in the short-term. When you do this, each stumbling block becomes an opportunity to grow and evolve.

Improved resilience isn't just as simple as looking on the bright side when bad things happen. Let's say I am having a really amazing day—one of the best days of the year. I'll tell my best friends and maybe my parents. Perhaps, I'll mention it in conversation with others if it comes up, but it's just a short mention, a blip on the timeline of the day. Conversely, if I have a bad day...I tell everybody. I explain every single gory detail of that rotten day, ad nauseam. I'll tell you every single detail: what people were wearing, the looks on their faces, what the cafeteria was serving that day...I may even provide sound effects to help orchestrate the terror of it all. I can talk about it for hours. Heck, years down the line I might even revive that story to tell again in all its awful glory. Want to hear about a bad day I had in November, 2002? I am more than willing to tell you, but I'll spare you.

Barbara Fredrickson, a professor of psychology and modern leader in the study of positivity, found that previous positive activities prepare us to better manage future stressful situations effectively. Negative events take up more of our brain space. Fredrickson found you need at least three positive experiences to counteract one negative incident.[17][18] You need these positive experiences to serve as a buffer; otherwise, negative emotions will keep you from problem-solving and long-term thinking. If we haven't built a solid bank of positive events and actions, we are more likely to be overcome by negative ones.

I didn't realize just how much building my positivity bank account had improved my ability to cope until my apartment flooded earlier this year. I came home to find my entire living room drenched, my filming equipment ruined, and some priceless heirlooms demolished. In this moment of chaos, I found myself surprisingly calm. I realized that getting stressed-out or angry over it wasn't going to fix it. It also wasn't going to give me any of the answers I needed. So even though I definitely felt stressed-out (stress is somewhat inevitable in these types of situations), I kept that sensation to a minimum. I instead found myself investing all that extra nervous energy into finding solutions. When I spoke to my building manager, I remember his response. "Usually people get very angry and that just makes resolving the situation even more challenging." Pause. Not only does useless negativity wear us out, it keeps us from moving forward.

> **How to Build a Positivity Bank Account**
>
> Keep track of positive things that happen in your life in a journal or spreadsheet. When stressful things happen you'll have a premade list of positive things in your life to draw on to help you through.

POSITIVE THINKING HELPS YOU RECOGNIZE OPPORTUNITIES

In one of my favorite episodes of the popular documentary series *The Experiments*,[19] Darren Brown does a series of experiments to better understand what makes people lucky. In one of these tests of kismet, Brown creates several "lucky" situations for a supposedly unlucky individual, Wayne. First, Brown sends a fake scratch-off prize card to Wayne in the mail. If Wayne would just give that lucky card a scratchety-scratch, he'd find that he's won a brand spankin' new TV. What does Wayne do? He throws the scratch card in the garbage. Next a fake interviewer is placed on the street offering a cash prize to anyone who could answer "today's special question." Brown designed this question specifically for Wayne. It would have been a piece of delicious, free money-cake for him to answer. However, Wayne pushes off the interviewer claiming he's "too busy" and quickly moves on. In the final test, fifty dollars is left smack dab in the middle of Wayne's path home from work. Wayne manages to walk home but completely ignore the money—even though it was directly in his line of sight.

I found this whole series of events fascinating, and a harsh reminder of one truth: "You create your own destiny." Through our actions and choices, we start to perpetuate the reality we think we deserve. In Wayne's case, he assumed unpredictable situations can only have a negative result. Therefore he avoided anything that wouldn't be a guaranteed success. Wayne no longer looked for opportunities, because he had convinced himself they didn't exist. When you take on negative attitudes, you restrict your access to life's advantages on a day-to-day basis by refusing to acknowledge your potential skills, engage with the community, and/or take risks. Simply put, you can't expect to fly, if you're afraid to leave the ground.

In another experiment,[20] the impact of positive emotions on the brain were tested. Subjects were divided into five groups and shown different clips of people that were each chosen to trigger a specific emotion. After viewing the clips, they were asked to imagine themselves in a similar situation and write down how they would react. Those who were exposed to clips showing positive emotions wrote down significantly higher number of actions they could take. Now this area of research is fairly new, but it goes to show that if we recognize and experience more happy things each day, we'll also recognize and acknowledge additional opportunities. You'll reach a little bit harder for the stars, because they simply won't feel so far away. I look at it this way: your ability to achieve a goal is directly related to how much you believe that goal is attainable.

When I was a teenage rebel, I focused on the negative. I didn't believe I was able or capable of becoming anything more than what I was. My own fear held me back from recognizing not only opportunities, but also my own talents. I believed I was worthless, and as a result that's what I became. It's amazing how in a few short years I was able to completely turn my life around, create lasting meaningful relationships, and find myself on a journey to the best me

I could be. It wasn't because I was destined to be a special story to be told in a Chicken Soup for the Soul storybook, it was because I worked hard to create a more positive lifestyle. In the following chapters, we'll address how you too can build positive habits to help you live your happiest, healthiest, and most fruitful life.

CHAPTER 2

IDENTITY: REALIZING YOU'RE DIFFERENT AND BECOMING SELF-AWARE

"Remember always that you not only have the right to be an individual, you have an obligation to be one."

—Eleanor Roosevelt

At age six, I remember sneaking into the kitchen and stealing some cookies to snack on before dinner. My father had told me several times that under no circumstance was I to have any of those sweet, chocolate morsel-filled biscuits before dinner. What he didn't know couldn't hurt him, right? As I found my way to the staircase, there were only a few carpet-covered wood stairs separating me from sweet success and even sweeter celebration. I had pulled off my heist. Victory was to be mine.

As I rounded the end of the banister, mere footsteps from my room, I found myself face-to-face with my father. I had pulled my shirt up, securing it there with my teeth, to form a MacGyver like sling for my stolen desserts. As I looked at him, my mouth gaped open, sending my shirt and the forbidden treats it contained tumbling down to the white carpet below. Having kept the cookies close to my chest, their little chocolate chips had melted. As they rolled across the tufted ground, they left streaks of brown goo behind them.

"*Anna!*" my father screamed, and this was followed with a few choice words not appropriate for this book or most public settings. I should mention that my father had spent hours on end caring for this carpet, steam-cleaning it and making sure it was pristine. I had been caught not only stealing forbidden treats, but had also destroyed my father's domestic pride and joy. His brow was furrowed and his face was red. I was done for.

I burst into a fit of tears, an effort to distract my father from the disaster zone I had created. Despite my best efforts, it did not work. Not at all. I was sent to my room to calm down and sentenced to a spanking with the mixing spoon. This was the ultimate form of punishment in my household, right up there with when my mother would angrily take her shoe off, wave it in the air and threaten us when we fought too much during road trips.

In my room, I panicked. How was I to escape this torture? After thinking about it for a long time, I grabbed two story books from the shelf and went down to accept my punishment. I would take this torture head on.

"Dad, I am ready now." I said to my father looking him square in the eye. Mixing spoon in hand, he turned to give me a quick thwap. The spoon made a hard cracking noise, as if it has hit something solid. My dad burst out laughing.

"Anna, what the hell do you have in your pants?" I reached down the back of my pants to pull out my two storybooks. I had used them as armor. My Dad looked at me with a goofy grin and gave me a big hug. He simply couldn't be upset with me.

Even as a child I was an inventive problem-solver. It's simply who I was meant to be. Isn't it funny how it seems we spend most of childhood shaping our unique identity, and then most of our adulthood trying to hide from what makes us different? In this chapter, we'll discuss how our brain works to understand the world around us, how it makes each of us truly unique, and how to become more self-aware. We'll tackle coping skills for accepting our uniqueness and learn why it's not only ok, but beneficial to stand out.

HOW WE DEVELOP OUR IDENTITY

Our brains are like the perfect organizational expert from our favorite home and garden TV show—they love to put similar things into neatly organized boxes. This happens with just about every type of information our fantabulous little noggin collects—experiences, emotions, and more. Your brain gets the same feeling grouping people that I get thinking about a shirtless sexy man holding sheet cake and telling me, "I just want to give you a back rub and hear about your day." When you see a person, your brain goes straight into analysis mode, making observations about their actions, appearance, demeanor, and more. Within as little as seconds, that relative stranger has been filed away by your subconscious in a pretty little box of supposedly similar things.

Our mental storage boxes are called "schema." It's basically a fancy science-y way of referring to a generalization about a group of people, places, situation and more. Stereotypes exist for a reason: it's just your brain trying to keep your thoughts tidy. Think about it. Every thought you have ever had is being organized and sorted into its perfect place. Everything in its box. I often wonder how my brain can be an ultimate store of all of this information, but still cannot effectively remind me to clean my house, buy toilet paper, or do my taxes.

These schemas also help us define ourselves and how we should react to things. Schema that characterize how we view ourselves are called self-schema. When I first started researching self-schema, I had a huge identity crisis. *Who am I?* I don't even know who I am. However, a few deep breaths and fifteen hours of reading Wikipedia pages with no relation to this book at all, I realized the obvious. I am who I am.

Your strongest self-schemas are always going to be the first things you use to describe yourself to a stranger. So for example, I am a beautiful, fearless, loud-mouthed woman. I care about the people around me deeply, but I am afraid of getting hurt. I am even more scared of failing. I work really hard, and I try every day to make the world happier. You will always know where you stand with me, and I value honesty more than anything else.

If we take a look at this blurb, we can see it not only defines who I am, but also helps my brain predict how I might react to certain situations and how I might engage with my community. Your brain is basically labeling a box of what you are, and on a day-to-day basis it helps you make decisions that fit neatly and comfortably in that box.

These perceptions of ourselves begin to develop as soon as we are born and are as unique as our experiences, environment, looks, and thoughts are. When people say "Speak your truth," the truth they are talking about is this pure definition of who you are. It's how you see your bodies, interests, personality, and behaviors.

They also often become self-perpetuating, meaning that we make choices that continue to reinforce how we have already defined ourselves. For example, if you identify as an extrovert, your mind is going to remind you that I need people to feel complete. It's going to give you the warm fuzzies when you get invited to a party or event. In the same vein of thought, if you spend too much time alone, it might trigger emotions such as loneliness, to remind you that you need to get out of the house and see some people.

These facts and tidbits about who we are get stored in the amygdala, or the emotional parts of our brain. Which means what we believe about ourselves doesn't have to be logical or factual. It simply has to be a pattern. When I was younger, I thought I was ugly. Not just kind of ugly—I thought I was hideous. At one point, I even gave up on grooming, because what was the point? I was a fugly teenager, I'd be a fugly adult. There was no point working on the parts of myself that couldn't be fixed.

I developed this self-definition because I was surrounded by friends, TV shows, and random strangers who constantly reminded me that because I was fat, I was also ugly. In my brain, the words fat and ugly were stored in the same box. For a long time, the two words were completely interchangeable for me. It took mentally redefining the word "fat" to help my brain begin to accept that I could identify as both fat and beautiful. Fat was no longer synonymous with ugly.

Now, changing how we see ourselves outright can be like climbing a mountain in flip-flops—painful and nearly impossible. But have no fear: adapting a schema is something our brain does all the time. Your identity evolves, based on the situations you put yourself in, your interactions with others, and how you feel about yourself.[21] I've had many women tell me that seeing my images has helped them see the beauty in who they are. At first I was like, "Lies!" How is that even possible?! They're just photos. However once I researched how the brain works, it made perfect sense.

The brain sees things bound together. In this case we'll use "fat and ugly," but usually in our brains things are much more complex. Now when you see an images of a woman like me and see them as being "fat and *beautiful*," your brain gets frustrated. Now the first time it happens, your brain might do just like all my ex-boyfriends, and make excuses for it. However if you continue to expose yourself to this cognitive dissonance, it will force your schema to evolve.

Our brain will be like: "Hold up. Trying to group these two things together isn't working anymore. They need to break up." Since these two things can no longer be fit into the same pretty little box, your mind will just have to go down to the basement (of your subconscious) and get another box. But the brain will only do this if it feels uncomfortable enough, often enough, to make that change. To change who we are, we must first challenge who we are.

How to Recognize Your Self-Schema

1. Start with the question—"Who am I?"

2. Answer honestly as you see yourself, not as you want the world to see you.

3. List the first twenty things that come to your mind, regardless of the connotation.

4. Group the list into key themes—these are most likely your core self-schema.

YOU ARE UNIQUE

Once you begin to understand how schemas are formed, it became apparent that each and every one of us is unique—just as our experiences, memories, emotions and bodies are unique. One of the biggest and most beneficial things you can learn in life is to embrace, rather than fear, this difference. We often over-focus on the benefits of sameness—no one gets bullied for not standing out. But by the same token, no one truly succeeds *without* standing out.

Let's say you meet two people today. One of them is unlike any person you've ever met. That person is fascinatingly different. The other is just like someone you already know. Which do you think you will remember more? Which do you think you might tell your friends about meeting?

Since your brain likes so much to group things, it's likely you will remember the unique person solely because they are, well, unique. Your brain had to make space in the attic for a whole new special crate just for them. You'll probably vividly recall little details about them—silly things like the color of their shoelaces or the way they pronounce a certain word. Anything your human supercomputer has latched onto as different from the norm. And the other individual? The one with similar traits to someone you've already met? They'll just get added to the same box as your existing friend. Other than that, you'll probably forget most things about them.

I once was at a business conference where individuals were presenting on creativity and technology. There were amazing speakers from the most innovative companies in the world like Google, Facebook, and more. However, if you asked me about what any of them presented on, I couldn't tell you. In my brain, they've all been lumped together into one box probably labeled something like "technology presenters who wear suits and talk about the future."

However, toward the end of the day, I remember one of the final speakers, Dave Trott, who was starting his presentation. As he took the stage, he dragged behind him an old, worn overhead projector and a stack of clear transfers. Instead of the typical business PowerPoint, he presented to us using handwritten information on those clear plastic sheets. The point of his presentation was to convince of one thing and one thing only: that being different makes you memorable. He wanted us to create a schema unique to him. It's been three years since that conference, and I can still remember that presentation clear as day. Mr. Trott was right: you never forget someone who dares to stand out.

Embracing and allowing your uniqueness to shine has some major benefits, beyond just being memorable. Once you know yourself, you can more easily communicate your needs, simply because they are more fully-formed. You are acknowledging them regularly. Decision-making becomes easier because the hesitation to choose based on your community's reaction is removed. In line with this thinking, you feel less guilt or regret as a result of those choices. You have a clearer vision of who you are, your goals, and the daily progress you are making toward them.

If embracing uniqueness is so beneficial to us, why is it so hard to do? Research shows that humans derive some pleasure from fitting in.[22] Conformity sometimes serves as an emotional proxy for one of our most basic human desires—belonging. When we think we belong somewhere, we feel connectedness to a group through a common goal and experience. We are happiest when we feel we truly belong, and find communities that embrace as we are.

However, at times, we convince ourselves that changing who we really are to fit into a community that may not be right for us will give us the same feeling as belonging. We make ourselves blend in, and we do it at any cost. Adapting our behaviors is a double-edged sword. We may feel like we belong, but we will also carry a constant fear that we are not deserving of this acceptance. It's that nagging fear that if someone knew the real us—they wouldn't like us. When we conform, we are doing so for short-term gains at the cost of our long-term happiness.

Embracing our individuality starts with self-awareness, or conscious knowledge of our own character, feelings, motives, and desires.[23] To successfully be self-aware, we must not only better understand how we see ourselves, but also take in how others perceive us.[24] Who we are becomes a delicate mix of these two perspectives.

GETTING TO KNOW YOURSELF

Over the course of my life, I've been through a lot. I've endured horrors that I hope no one else ever experiences. I've rebuilt myself. I've conquered fears. I've adapted my emotions of anger and frustration into ones of understanding and patience. I've done hundreds of things people have told me I will never be able to do. Every day, I look in the mirror and I see this. It kills me that so many other people don't do the same. They see their faults and problems. They see their ugliness and pain. They see someone else's definition of who they are, because they haven't made time to define themselves.

Finding myself and my place in this world was a journey— and a hard one at that. I don't want you to think any of this will be easy. You will have to fight yourself to find yourself. Every time you hesitate or doubt something you wanted to try based on what you think you are allowed to experience, you have to force yourself to try and do it anyways. Gradually, it becomes habit. The fear drops away and a fresh confidence can grow in its place. Soon those things that terrified you, that once felt out of your reach, become things that make you feel powerful. Eventually, you see yourself in actions rather than in words. You see beauty in who you are, and not in the words strangers might use to describe you.

Discovering who you are is a process. You have to make time and emotional space to dig under all the layers of "what you should be" to discover who you could be. Slowly, you begin to understand what you want in life, what causes you to do the things you do, and what your emotions are trying to tell you. Begin with a journal to track your feelings. Set goals you want to achieve, so that when you are faced with life decisions you can always check in and make the right choices for your future self. Lastly, make time every day to get away from the noise of the world to just think about who you are, where you are going, and what you have accomplished so far.

Tasha Eurich, author of *Insight*,[25] studied a group of individuals who were proven to be successfully self-aware. Her research resulted in some interesting results. Often when a situation goes awry we ask ourselves, "Why?" Why didn't I get this job? Why didn't I get asked to prom? Why do I feel alone? The word "why" focuses our attention on assessing past decisions and events. Through this process, we expect to discover a reason for our current situation. However, our minds are fickle beasts, our memory isn't perfect, and much of the information we use to make decisions lives in the messy basement of our brains (our subconscious).

When we ask ourselves "why," we are forcing ourselves to rehash a situation that has already passed and that we likely have a skewed perspective on, looking to discover a detail we can't change and hoping this knowledge will make us happier in the future. If this sounds unrealistic, it's because it is. This type of introspection can make us stressed-out. It can depress us. Even worse, it delays our ability to solve problems. We literally become trapped in our own self-analysis of our history. We can't move forward.

I remember having dinner with a friend where we discussed our pasts. We both had similar disadvantages and challenges as kids. My dinner partner, once recognizing we had a similar history, asked me how I had managed to become successful despite it all. As we continued to discuss each event and dissect how my choices had netted me in increasingly better positions, I began to notice a pattern.

Every time a major incident happened, I always asked myself what I could do to make it better. With each setback I developed some new learning about myself that would motivate my next action in life. After years of working hard to always find ways to be better and overcome my rebellious past, I developed the unwavering belief that the best thing I could learn from today was what I needed to do tomorrow to improve. In fact, for the last ten years I have been asking myself that same question nearly every day. What can I do tomorrow, this month, this year to make tomorrow better than today?

Interestingly enough, Eurich's research found that those who receive the most value from self-awareness are those who analyze their lives using the word "what."[26] By phrasing questions when self-analyzing using "what," we are asking ourselves to critically think about our values, needs, and wants and establish what we need to do to make them a reality. This makes us better able to handle tough situations, because we're always focused on taking a future action and less likely to get bogged down by whatever terrible, no-good, rotten past events and mistakes we might make along the journey. We're letting them go instead of constantly digging through garbage (bad events), hoping to a find a nugget of gold (an amazing insight or life direction).

Activities to Increase Your Self-Awareness

1. Keep a journal of your emotions and feelings and look for patterns in your behavior.

2. Set goals to help center your growth and development around an objective.

3. Choose "what" versus "why" when applying critical introspection.

HOW OTHER PEOPLE SEE YOU

When I took my very first corporate job, I had trouble transitioning from "cool co-ed Anna" to formal, full suit-wearing "Ms. O'Brien." I treated my cubicle much like one would treat their fifth-grade locker: I covered the walls in *Teen Beat* posters of JTT. Yes, this was ten years after JTT's star had peaked. I painted my nails at my desk, put googly eyes on the office plants, and listened to my music out loud for all to hear. I even went so far as to come in one weekend and give my cube a *Trading Spaces* (does anyone remember that show?) makeover, complete with hanging lanterns and a tapestry pinned up like wallpaper. I thought I was being whimsical and funny. What I was doing was committing career suicide.

I remember when HR called me into the office to talk about these cubicle antics. I had anticipated good news—

maybe even a promotion. I had made so much effort to liven up our humdrum office floor, and I expected them to be grateful. I was wrong. The office found me annoying, distracting, and unfocused. Gulp. They didn't love me, they hated me. I was distraught. I needed to start looking for a new job. I was a failure. They were going to fire me any day.

I spent the next two weeks silently working at my desk. I didn't leave for lunch. I stayed late. I was terrified anytime someone senior walked over to my desk. Eventually my mentor at the time pulled me aside and helped me see the light. My HR manager hadn't told me those things to make me feel bad; she had told them to me to make me better. I was given feedback, but because of my own insecurities I had turned it into criticism.

Being able to receive feedback is crucial for becoming more self-aware and developing into the best version of ourselves. Take my office shenanigans. Obviously, I was young and I just wanted desperately to belong and be accepted in my new adult world. It wasn't that I was intentionally doing things wrong; I was simply misguided. In college, the likable people went to parties and dressed like they were always prepared to be a backup dancer in a rap video. I was mimicking that behavior and doing what totally professionally inexperienced me thought would help me belong. I needed feedback to correct my actions. It wasn't an attack, it was a gift.

When people give us feedback and we actually make changes, a funny thing happens. People respect us for it. As I began to apply my HR manager's feedback, I also began to repair those bridges I had burned with my loud music, colorful walls and childish antics. Just like I had learned as the original office party girl so many years ago, it is true that if we listen and take action on feedback regularly, we are more respected by our peers, are better leaders,[27] and deliver better results professionally.

Just like we have to learn how to receive feedback, giving feedback is also a skill. Let me tell you the painful truth— not all people were made to give feedback. When you find someone who can really offer insight, *never let them go*. Choose who you rely on for feedback very carefully. Personally, I look for people who have a reputation for being a good mentor to others or who have a history of career or life coaching.

Your first time hearing feedback you will probably react, much like I did, by internalizing and attaching emotions to the feedback the giver did not convey or mean. This is why I always choose someone I trust and who I feel will give me the benefit of the doubt if I overreact. Finding a mentor who, in the beginning, will let you react openly and help you work through those emotions is essential to progression. Always frame the situation first by letting them know upfront that this is a new experience for you and that asking for feedback is hard for you. You are still working on how to better learn about yourself from others. Let them know that becoming more self-aware is important to you—I was 100 percent honest in saying that I may not react well initially, and my openness helped my mentors prepare for and not take it personally when I got flustered.

It is important to acknowledge that not all feedback we receive is meaningful feedback. Sometimes feedback helps us to course-correct and recognize we are sacrificing our self and happiness to achieve a goal. When you receive feedback, always be thankful for the other person's perspective, but remember that you still have the power. You get to acknowledge and apply it, or you can choose to reject it. You are always in the driver's seat. Feedback just helps you understand where certain roads may lead.

Learning to take and apply feedback is something that only gets better with practice and is a lifelong pursuit. However, the more open we are to receiving feedback, the more opportunities we will have for growth. There have been times I have received feedback that taught me things about myself I would have never realized on my own. There have also been times where feedback helped me realize that the changes I need to make to achieve a certain goal weren't worth it. Feedback is simply another feed of information to help us learn about ourselves, and we can use it to make more informed decisions about what will make us happy.

How to Successfully Ask for Feedback

1. Come with Goals: Let the person you're asking feedback from know what you are hoping to achieve from their assessment.

2. Focus on the Future: Ask for feedback about what you can do better in the future instead of dissecting the validity of past behavior.

3. Actively Listen: Let the person share their entire feedback before reacting. This is not only respectful to the feedback-giver, but also makes it easier for them to give you feedback.

4. Ask for Clarity: Don't be afraid to ask for examples or more details if feedback is unclear or doesn't make sense to you. Write down key ideas or themes to follow up on.

5. Express Gratitude: Giving feedback is as hard as getting it, so make sure to let your feedback-giver know how much you appreciate their time.

CHAPTER 3

COMPARISON: THE GOOD, THE BAD, AND THE UGLY

"Always be a first-rate version of yourself, instead of a second-rate version of somebody else."

—Judy Garland

Sometimes it feels like we have to fight against treating each day as some sort of judged competition. It can feel like our brain wants to analyze every action we take, every movement we make, and every thought we think and tally them on some sort of giant scorecard that equals the success of our lives. Here's your brain's sports announcer, the play-by-play:

> "We're coming at you live, where Anna O'Brien is just taking the 'Arena of Life' floor. Anna will be doing a complicated 'business lady turned social media star' routine, with a surprise author flip. Anna starts her routine. So far, we're seeing a lot of what we expect here at today's competition. She starts off with the morning dog-walk, followed by a smooth transition into a 'talking to neighbors and petting her dog' combination. A solid four points for opening the door

for an older woman. She racks up another three for creating a well-thought-out PowerPoint. In a surprise turn of events, Anna has racked up an impressive amount of difficulty points by finally doing those dirty dishes in the sink while also talking her best friend through a bad day. However, she's now taken a bit of a performance hit for playing Tetris on her phone instead of answering work emails. Anna needs to get refocused on her routine if she hopes to even qualify for tomorrow's existence. We'll have final results after the eyes shut. Back to you, Roberta!"

You might be sitting there scratching your head, reading this and thinking, "Anna, this is ridiculous." And you're right, it is. There is no scorecard in life. There is no team of highly trained life experts assessing your every choice, trying to decide a perfect number value to assign to your life effort today, or any day really. No one is going to hold up a placard with your worth at the end of each day.

If there is no scorecard to life, why do we often feel like we are constantly in a competition with ourselves, with others, and with the world around us? In this chapter we will dissect how unnecessary comparison leads us to treat our lives like a competition. This, in turn, fuels negative self-talk. I'll share methods I use to remove competition from my life and reduce unnecessary comparison. We'll also dissect how not all comparisons are bad. (Some even help us grow!) Lastly, I'll share tricks I use to reduce competitiveness in my own life.

LIFE IS NOT A COMPETITION

When I was in middle school, you might be shocked to learn I played basketball. I was tall and a decent rebounder, but I could not get that ball to go in the basket to save my life. Basketball, like any competition, had a clear goal: get that orange sphere through the swooshy net the most in the time allotted. So while I was terrible at scoring, I tried to give it my all in defense. I should note that in middle school I was significantly taller than everyone around me, and built like a monster truck. I also let my mother cut my hair into a super feminine and attractive bowl cut, and wore a pair of 1980s coke bottle glasses with a nifty elastic band. I most definitely looked like a scary forty-year-old librarian who was going to punish you for returning your books late. Intimidation is what I brought to the court.

No matter how badass I might have looked, and how much muscle I could bring to the party, I knew there were a clear set of boundaries and rules I had to follow. When you think of something you can "win," like my basketball game, there's a clear pattern. Think about it. Competitions have a clear objective, defined before the contest begins, which participants are trying to achieve. The game begins with a clear set of rules you have to follow while trying to achieve the task at hand. And from the time the match begins, your opposition is clearly defined; you know who or what you're competing against. Lastly, you know when it will all end; the time elapses or the objective is achieved which signals we're no longer competing and the game is over. Think about your life. It doesn't fit so well into that architecture, now does it?

Life is not a competition. Unlike a game of basketball we don't start life knowing what we are trying to achieve. This might sound terrifying. What do you mean my purpose isn't clear from day one? But think about it, we don't pop out of our mother's womb with a roadmap to what we need to achieve for the next ninety-odd years of living. Instead we are built with the raw tools required to discover what we can make of our lives. In this way life is less like a game and more like a work of art. Part of the joy of living is getting to define just what kind of awesome you want to add to the world. Imagine if we didn't get to choose where we were headed, that wouldn't be as much fun, now would it?

Many would argue life does have a set of rules, or a moral code. Don't steal your best friend's man, no matter how fine he is. Don't kill your neighbors who like to party at 3 a.m. on a Tuesday. Don't gossip about Cindy's deviated septum surgery. However, this code, while applicable most of the time, isn't set in stone. Moral guides are subject to adapt or change based on the context of the situation. Take, for example, lying. Most people would argue lying is a bad thing, and that we should all be truthful. However, if a dangerous person demanded your home address, would it be wrong if you lied, giving them a false address to protect yourself? In this way many of the moral codes we rely on are not rules, but rather guides to living a more righteous life.

Much like our moral code, our opposition in life is often contextual. As a child you might feel like your competition is your annoying brother or sister. As a teenager it might be a student from a different clique. As an adult it might be a coworker who's up for the same promotion. But it's not that simple, now is it? You might feel like you're competing with multiple people for multiple things all at once, based on different facets of our life. You might feel you need to have a better lasagna recipe than Suzy, while also beating Roger for the promotion at work, while also challenging Margaret for captain of your rec soccer league, while also convincing your boyfriend to settle down with you. If that sentence seems exhausting, it's because it is. The people in life who challenge us are ever-changing and totally unpredictable.

Lastly, we don't know when our game is going to end. No, I am not making a morbid reference to death. Does the game end when we die? Or does it end when we achieve a certain number of life milestones? Heck, we don't even know when the game started. I hardly think the first thing we think popping into this bright beautiful world is, "So glad to be out of that woman's uterus—I'm ready for this. Game on."

You wouldn't play a game that has no clear objective, unclear rules, an ever-changing cast of competitors. So why do we push so hard to treat life as if it's some grand event we must win?

GETTING OUT OF THE GAME

In school, we're taught to compete to be the best. In the workplace, we're all fighting for that next promotion. It's hard not to constantly feel in competition with the world around you. These milestones in our lives are often framed in the context of others. It's not, "I need to be the best." Instead, we are taught we must beat everyone else to be the best. We're led to believe the competition is not only a good thing, but necessary to motivate us to be our best. We are taught that excellence can only be achieved through winning.

The sad part is when our only focus is on the win, we lose the joy of the moments in life for what they are. Alfie Kohn, an experienced researcher of human behavior, put it best: "The point isn't to paint or read or design a science experiment, but to win. The act of painting, reading, or designing is thereby devalued in [our] mind." How often we trade the joy of living for various trophies and titles, and then wonder why, when surrounded by all these badges of success, we feel unhappy. You might be asking yourself, "How do I step out of the 'game' when everything around me feels like it's created to drive competition?"

Changing the way we think about comparison and competition is hard, but not impossible. The first step is to recognize and acknowledge how you currently measure your personal success against others. The big ways we create competition are easy to recognize because they usually center around potential life milestones. For example, weddings, having kids, and advancing at work always seem to involve a ton of competition. You can't just get married, you have to have the perfect wedding with the best band and the perfect dress. Your kids need to be top performers, and you have to give them a head start so they, like you, can win. You need to keep beating out everyone around you and do anything to ensure you get the new promotion.

These major stages of life are fraught with competition and are a good place to start acknowledging its presence in your life. When you make a conscious effort to recognize where you engage in this "winning over living" mentality in your life, you'll likely realize you're in way more sparring matches than you thought. Do you really need to battle to bake the best cupcakes? Is it really that important to reign as top vocalist at after-work karaoke? Probably not, but once we get caught in the competitive vortex we are pretty good at turning the dumbest and most meaningless things into opportunities to win. But why do we do this?

Research on how the brain processes victory shows that winning gives us a temporary high by releasing dopamine, the "feel-good" chemical. Dopamine is the neurotransmitter that's responsible for that feeling of pleasure. The chemical release comes from a result of our identity being associated with a schema we have defined in our brain as important. Basically, the brain likes when we get to put ourselves into pretty boxes. However this emotional rush is temporary and will not persist forever.

As a result, we often find ourselves using comparisons in our day-to-day life to try and correct disappointment and get us back to the original high we experienced with our achievement. For example, you might compare yourself with the person you beat for a promotion and highlight how your skills are superior to theirs. This is called a downward comparison. Similarly, when you don't win, you might make negative comparisons with the intention of motivating yourself to potentially achieve more. This is called an upward comparison. While comparisons can be helpful in personal development, when overused they can cause self-doubt, burnout, and feelings of worthlessness.

Downward Comparisons

We all want to be cool in our youth. Do you remember all the things we got into just because everyone else was into them? Uggs. Beanie Babies. Boy Bands. Whatever was popular at the moment, we wanted. Do you remember the girl at your high school (I am certain everyone had one) who had magically found her way to the epicenter of cool? She was the oracle or popularity. She decided what was in, for how long, and when it was out. If you've seen *Mean Girls* you know what I am talking about. Every high school has a Regina George.

My high school was no exception. Our high school prophetess of popularity was Amanda Scott. (That's not her real name, because I'm a nice person.) I wanted Amanda to like me so badly. I thought maybe if she knew all the hard things I was dealing with at home that she would befriend me or at least be kinder to me. So I wrote Amanda a note. I told her absolutely everything I was going through—every gory detail. I told her how sad I was. I told her how much I looked up to her. I poured my soul out onto that college-ruled piece of paper, slid it into her locker, and waited.

I waited and waited and waited. I waited so long I thought I was going to drop dead due to a mix of anxiety and anticipation. Finally, when I walked into the hallway, Amanda pulled me aside and thanked me for my note. Nothing more. That was it. I has poured my entire life out in lead and tears and all she could say was "Thanks?" I was hurt and confused, but figured that was the end of it all. However, this is high school. It would not end there.

Later that day, while walking to my next class I overheard Amanda talking to another girl. I listened closely. Call it intuition or call it paranoia—I knew they were talking about me. Amanda's hair perfectly bounced to the side as she casually said to her minion, "I may be have been having a rough time, but at least I am not putting notes in people's lockers about it." She laughed. They laughed. I died inside.

Amanda had used my vulnerability as a way to bolster her perceived stability.

Amanda's comments about my note provide a perfect example of what sociologists call downward comparison. Downward comparisons are when you compare yourself to someone you perceive is inferior to, or less fortunate than, you in some way. It's easy to make Amanda into a villain (because she really was a garbage human being to do such a thing), but the reality is we have all used downward comparisons to make ourselves feel better. I personally do it most often when indulging in a juicy marathon of reality TV. I can't help but give myself a little pat on the back for never having tried to pull a frenemy's hair out at a French restaurant, stolen cheap vodka from my work, or stayed in a relationship with a guy who continuously cheats on me.

Sometimes it just feels so good to recognize we're a little bit better off than someone else. When we make these types of comparisons, as we discussed earlier, our brain releases dopamine which improves our self-worth temporarily. Have you ever tried to stay awake on energy drinks instead of taking a nap? You might stay up, but you're a jittery mess and definitely less than your best. We use downward comparisons much like we use caffeine. They give us a brief jolt of positive energy when we feel down, to help us keep going. The problem is they also often prolong us from solving the underlying issues causing us to feel frustrated with our lives. Just like drinking caffeine instead of sleeping, if we only rely on downward comparisons to make us feel better it can lead to emotional exhaustion and even burnout.

Upward Comparisons

When I was in elementary school, I somehow got it into my head that I was meant to be a cheerleader. Let's quickly unpack why this was not likely my ideal destiny. While I have always been a very enthusiastic individual, I am not a sports fan. In fact, I genuinely don't understand why people get excited about watching people push, kick, or throw a ball from one side of a rectangle to the other. Wanna shoot some hoops? I'm game. Want to watch someone else shoot hoops, and I'll be over here playing *Super Mario Brothers* on my Gameboy until the monotony is over.

On top of that, even as a little kid I have always been my own rainbow of sorts. You know when you see videos of elementary school choral concerts and there's just one kid on stage doing whatever they feel like, living their best life. I was 100 percent that kid. I never marched well to the beat of anyone else's drum but my own. So how I got it in my mind that I was a perfect fit for a recreational activity, cheering on something I hated to watch, in a manner where uniformity was not only encouraged, but required, I will never know.

When cheerleader tryouts rolled around, this girl was ready for battle. My hair was high, my shirt was bright, and I was ready to yell while waving my arms around enthusiastically. I walked into a room of girls practicing backbends, tumbling and stretching out in the splits. Fast forward two hours, ten questionable "high" kicks, and a pike jump that was pretty much me touching my toes and doing a bunny hop at the same time later. It was clear I was not meant to be a cheerleader.

I remember driving home from the auditions with my heart crushed. I am sure you've been there before, where you try for something you really want and don't just fall down— you get crushed. I sat there, scrunched down in my car seat thinking about what a pathetic loser I was and how my life had no meaning because I wasn't even able to make the cheerleading squad. All I could do was run through my head all the things I couldn't do. I struggled to learn the routine, I couldn't do a backbend, and my "pep" was more of an awkward wheeze of exhaustion than a motivator. Obviously I was a worthless human.

My reaction to cheerleader status rejection is a classic example of a negative upward comparison. Upward comparisons are when you compare yourself to someone with greater skills or higher status than yourself. These comparisons are rarely unbiased. We often take a weak attribute about ourselves (cheerleading) and compare it to the strongest quality of someone else. As a result these types of comparisons more often than not make us feel unhappy with our abilities and ourselves.

Now it should be mentioned that you can use upward comparisons to motivate yourself to make changes in your life and progress toward your goals. For example, when you look up to someone, you might acknowledge areas you need to work on to achieve a similar level or success. However, more often than not, the upward comparisons we do make are unfair to ourselves.

It seems we are trained to recognize all the things we aren't versus all the things we are. In many ways this becomes a mental pattern of constantly acknowledging other skills, and being remorseful that we are not similarly talented. In this way, upward comparisons foster feelings of helplessness, jealousy, and inferiority, which can jeopardize our happiness and our identity. Who are we when we only define ourselves in the strengths of others?

REMOVING UNNECESSARY COMPARISON FROM YOUR LIFE

Not all comparisons are bad. In fact, comparisons can be a motivator to help us achieve goals, try new things, and grow as a person. When used effectively, both upward and downward comparisons can be helpful. That said, comparisons are often used more than necessary, to the point that they affect our mental health. Simply stated, you can benefit from comparing yourself to others less. Here are five easy ways I recommend reducing the number of unnecessary comparisons in your life.

The first step to correcting any behavior is to acknowledge when and how often it happens. It might seem like a small thing, but becoming aware of just how often you compare yourself to others can help you better understand why you do it. Making an effort to recognize when you are rating yourself against another is the first step toward correcting this potentially toxic behavior.

As you begin to acknowledge when you evaluate yourself against someone else, it is likely you will notice patterns in your behaviors, situations, or even people that trigger your need to compare. When you recognize these trends, reflecting on the root cause can help you to re-architect your response. Additionally, you might find that certain things encourage you to compare yourself to others and are toxic to your own happiness. Removing yourself from them (as much as possible) can help limit your desire to compete while also improving your overall self-worth.

For those situations where you can't remove yourself and comparison seems inevitable, try to reframe comparative phrases to focus on you. When you have thoughts that stack yourself up against someone else, try to think how you could reframe the thought to be more about you and less about someone else. For example, you might think, "Cindy is way more popular me. She is so lovable and her sweat smells like gumdrops." Phrased this way, the majority of your mental space is focused on how Cindy is so awesome. When you reframe the phrase to be about yourself and how you want your life to improve, you might say, "I want to have more friends, so I need to work on getting out of my comfort zone and meeting new people." Here we see that by turning the phrase to be about ourselves we not only remove the comparison, but also are more likely to work toward improving ourselves.

Another way to manage chronic comparison is to try and humanize the situation. While it might seem like nitpicking, acknowledging a person's human tendencies can help us take them off of a golden pedestal. This is especially helpful for those who regularly put themselves down when comparing themselves to others. For example, you might say that, "Ashley is the smartest girl in class and there is no way I will ever be as smart." In this way, you put Ashley on a pedestal because of her intelligence. Looking more closely at Ashley, you might notice that she is socially awkward and has a hard time making friends. In this way you humanize Ashley by acknowledging she has amazing strengths (like being super smart), but there are also things she is weak in (social interaction). You can then also apply the same principle to yourself. Take time to acknowledge that while you are weak in the area you are comparing to another, there might be other areas where you are strong.

Lastly, one of my favorite ways to remove comparison from my life is to engage in activities that you don't intend to ever be the best at. This might sound crazy, but by starting an activity or hobby from scratch we create a blank slate. If you enter that blank slate with the goal of it not being something you need to be good at you remove the pressure to succeed from the onset. Here you can explore a new skill freely and focus on the act of doing rather than winning. This activity can become a much needed reprieve from your day-to-day life—your comparison free zone. Additionally when you focus on the experience versus the outcome, it allows you to subconsciously reconnect with what you enjoy doing versus what you feel pressure to do well at.

Five Ways to Reduce Comparison

1. Acknowledge: Take time to mentally note or keep a journal of when you make comparisons in your day-to-day life.

2. Look for Triggers: Be on the lookout for people, places, and things that trigger you to compare yourself. Cut out these negative influences to reduce your pressure to compete.

3. Reframe Comparisons: Turn comparison thoughts into statements that put you and the goals you want to achieve at the forefront.

4. Humanize Comparisons: Even out the playing field by recognizing both the strengths and weaknesses of those you compare yourself to.

5. Try Something New: Try a new activity or hobby and put your focus on enjoying the activity versus being the best.

CHAPTER 4

SELF-LOVE: ACKNOWLEDGING YOUR WORTH

"Never bend your head. Always hold it high. Look the world straight in the face."

—Helen Keller

In 2012, I took a job in a technology startup as employee number twenty-something. Now for those of you only familiar with technology startups from TV shows and movies, it is not the party, double-polo-shirt wearing, popped-collar lifestyle it is often portrayed as. Instead it is long days, often sleepless nights and an ever growing list of demands you can never really keep up with. In the beginning it felt exciting, and the adrenaline (plus lots and lots of caffeine) helped me power through the crazy cocktail of fatigue and pressure. It made me feel powerful, and the high I got from creating something new and innovative made me feel invincible.

However, after about two years, I started to crack. I was sick all the time. I forfeited going to birthdays and weddings, to work on the next big assignment or to just sleep. Sleep was a luxury I could rarely afford. I never had time to see my friends. On the rare occasion I did, I would babble insistently on about my job. Work. Work. Workity work work. It was my everything. My emotions became tied to the success of my projects and the growth of the company. Numbers were up? I was having an amazing day. Software was on the blitz? Do not poke the bear. I'd given up on myself in favor of my career.

The signs were everywhere. My apartment was in a constant state of disarray. I was never home, so who cared if I lived in a giant pile of clothes dusted with the bags from take outs past? My shower schedule was based on when I had meetings. Big sit-down with a client? I showered. Otherwise I lived life as a greasy filth monkey; I was the adult version of Pigpen from *Charlie Brown*. Except my dirt cloud wasn't drawn in—it was real. My clothes followed suit. On the days we had clients, I dressed well—as if I was donning some sort of boss-lady superhero costume. Otherwise, I wandered into my office in leggings and some variation of a moderately clean T-shirt. I had taken myself completely out of my life. I had stopped taking care of myself and I was headed for a break down.

Maybe you've experienced something like this before, where you wake up and all the sudden everything seems one hundred times more difficult to do. Your body feels heavy, your mind feels like mush, and you have no motivation to do anything except play *Candy Crush* on your phone and cry. That's what ended up happening to me. I laid in my bed for two days straight, only getting up to go the bathroom. I thought I was depressed, but the doctor told me the truth—I was exhausted. I had put everyone else's needs in front of my own and in the end I'd lost the ability to take care of myself. I was depleted, worn-out, and practically used up. I needed to take better care of myself. I started my Instagram account as a way to force a little "me" time into my life. Some might call it vanity, but getting dressed every day became the time I invested in myself. It wasn't about PowerPoints or deadlines, it was about investing in myself and exploring my creativity. I'll admit at first I felt a teensy bit guilty about my indulgence. That quickly passed as I began to see that everyone was benefiting. I thought that if I cut back, work would fall apart. It didn't. Actually, by reducing the hours I worked and giving myself some mental space from my job, my work improved. I wasn't exhausted all the time and could think more clearly when completing tasks. This makes sense— research from Stanford University found that after about fifty hours of work, our productivity and output plummets.[28] I was able to get more done in less time because I was making fewer careless mistakes.

I had needlessly been worried people would see me as conceited. Instead they saw me as more committed to my job. Showing up well-groomed gave the appearance I was more committed to what I did. What I ultimately learned is that the more you care for yourself, the more you are able to care for and support the ones (and the work) you love. I wish I didn't need to have a breakdown to realize that.

I urge you, don't be like me. Don't learn the hard way. Today is just as good a day as any other day to start valuing you. The single greatest lesson I've learned (and ultimately the most difficult and painful as well) is that I matter. That it's ok to make a decision because it's the best choice for you. That you don't have to say yes to everything others ask of you. You cannot physically or mentally help anyone else until your own house is in order. In trying to please others you lose yourself; knowing who you are and what truly motivates you is only found by making the space for self-care in your life.

Like many new things, it's scary. It's hard. It's uncomfortable. However, in the end you walk away with the benefits of a strong sense of self. To quote *Game of Thrones*: "Once you know and own who you are, it can never be used against you." A person who loves themselves is a force to be reckoned with. In this chapter, we'll talk about how to develop a stronger sense of self through gratitude, talk about the importance of feelings all the feels, and introduce ways to recognize when you are in need of a little extra self-care.

SELF-LOVE IS NOT SELFISH

As mentioned before when I started to invest more in self-care, I felt selfish. Perhaps you too have felt greedy. Maybe you feel like you should instead be investing your time and energy helping inner-city kids paint culturally sensitive murals, knitting sweaters for cold grandmas or rescuing three-legged dogs. For some reason, and I really don't have a good explanation as to why, we've been trained to view taking care of our basic mental and physical needs as selfish. If I achieve one thing in this entire book, I hope it's to right that terrible wrong. You are worthy of self-love and care.

Think about a car. To keep a car running well, you need to change the oil regularly. You need to check the tires, test the brake pads, and sometimes even charge the battery. If you neglect doing these routine things, eventually your wonder wheels might overheat, break down or drive unpredictably. Sure, humans aren't machines, but the same logic applies to taking care of ourselves. If we don't take time to lovingly care for ourselves, we put ourselves at risk for a meltdown.

You really only have so much you can handle in a given day, month, year, life. Taking care of yourself isn't being selfish, it's actually making sure you can help many more people over a longer time period, by keeping your life in order. I know when I don't take care of myself, I turn into a grotesque prickly monster version of myself and the people around me have to deal with that. How is that helping anyone—adding another worn-out soul that needs uplifting to the mix? Running yourself into the ground to help others becomes pointless because this makes you into a burden to deal with in the process.

I love this quote from a piece *The New Yorker* did on the modernization of self-care. "When you endorse yourself as both vulnerable and worthy, especially when that endorsement feels hard, you can grant that same complex subjectivity to others, even to people whose needs and desires are different from your own."[29] By investing time in learning how to best care for and respect yourself, you also learn how to better do the same for others. People who practice self-love are more likely to celebrate the success of others and more willing to cheer them on in times of need.

If you make an effort to routinely make space for you and your own self-care, you can help others adapt to healthy behaviors by osmosis. Have you ever had lunch with a well-adjusted happy friend and they tell you about some new thing they are doing to find more peace in life? If you're like me, you spend the thirty minutes directly after the meal Googling said thing. If it helps them live a calmer life, maybe it will also help me. This ripple effect is a great example of how practicing self-love habits can help you set a good example to others, and help them discover self-love too. Showing people how you care for and love yourself when you get overwhelmed or stressed-out inspires them to evaluate how they too can better care for themselves. That's not so selfish now, is it?

FEEL ALL THE FEELS

So far in this chapter we've talked a lot about loving and caring for yourself. I want you to know that just because you care for yourself, it does not guarantee you will be happy all the time. The world would have you think you have to be a brilliant ray of golden sunshine all the dang time. Your smile should radiate happiness, and your eyes should have that sparkly joyful gleam. If not, you are seen as broken. What a completely unrealistic expectation this is. This a safe space, let's be real. Our days are usually a roller-coaster of emotions. Instead of being afraid of these changes in mood, embrace them. If you have a bad day at work and feel angry—that's ok. If someone breaks your heart—shed those tears. If a stranger gets red lipstick on your white suede jacket—pout and be annoyed. It's okay to feel upset something didn't go right.

People are complex beings, and we're not meant to be happy all the time. Shocker! Sometimes really bad things happen to really good people. Instead of getting frustrated about these emotions, welcome them as opportunities to improve your self-love. Emotions help us to recognize opportunities for change and to acknowledge where we still have to grow.

Emotions are expressed in three different ways. First is how we experience them and make a decision on how to react. This is called the cognitive component. Often when you feel overwhelmed, you feel tired and stressed. This is your body reacting to the experience, the physiological part of an emotion or what we commonly call "feelings." The third way emotions are expressed is by how we react to them, which is the behavioral component. How each of these parts of an emotion are experienced and used in how we express ourselves varies by person, culture, and community. Some people get angry and yell, other just take it to the floor and dance it out. However you experience those emotions, each of these components work together to drive you to take actions to improve your life.[30]

Let's say you go to meet a few friends for drinks. You arrive in a somewhat empty room and people jump out to surprise you for your birthday. Physiologically, you might feel the emotion of surprise by an increased heart rate, your muscles may tense up and then relax, and your body temperature might rise. Cognitively, you're experiencing the same emotion, but in a different way. Your brain is likely going to think through the emotion and use it to assess the situation, your surroundings, and what thoughts you have in regards to how it makes you feel. In this example, you might be trying to decide if this is a good surprise or a bad one.

You might also be setting expectations for the surprise party, whether it will be enjoyable or wondering if certain people will be in attendance. Some cognitive experiences could also trigger other emotions, like you might be happy because your friends created such a lovely party for you. You might react to this excitement by squealing out loud or giving a big bear hug to your friends who organized it. These are examples of how we process emotions using behaviors, our third component of the emotional expression.[31]

These emotional responses send out signals to ourselves and to others about who we are, what we enjoy, and what we find challenging. Respecting and allowing yourself to express emotions fully allows you to better understand your true preferences. It also helps others to learn our preferences. By expressing our emotions authentically, we organically create an environment that gets more and more pleasing over time. We are also protecting ourselves, as it will tell us when situations, people or places might threaten our long-term happiness. When we suppress our emotions because we are afraid other people won't like them or judge us for them, we put ourselves at risk of enduring unnecessary trauma, prolonging unhealthy relationships, or preventing necessary healing. Emotions are essential to improving our lives, and an important part of self-care is feeling all the feels and then using those emotions to make meaningful improvements to your life.

HOW TO PRACTICE SELF-LOVE

Before we jump into the nitty-gritty, I think it's important for you to understand why you might feel so negative about yourself in the first place. We talked a little bit in an earlier chapter about how our minds weigh negative information as more valuable than positive. This is called a negativity bias. Some researchers believe this was an evolutionary advantage.[32] In other words, negative information might have actually been more useful in making judgments that helped our ancestors survive. Whatever the reason, our brain is genetically hard-wired to give more thought and attention to a dissenting opinion.

Additionally, our brains are presented with millions of signals a day—too many, actually. Your brain can't process it all. Instead, your mind tries to focus only on the tasks at hand—or whatever you're actively thinking or doing. Have you ever pulled out your phone to look at your email or cute pictures of puppies cuddling with tigers and your friend had to physically startle you to get your attention? This is a great example of what's called "sensory gating." It's literally your mind turning off and tuning out of any unnecessary stimuli.[33] Your friend has to literally startle you to break through the gate by presenting a potential threat. What we learn from this is that if you're not focused on something and/or your body doesn't need to process that stimuli to survive, then your brain is probably ignoring it.

Now let's relate this to your own self-perception. If we view negative information as more important (and potentially related to our continued survival), it's more likely to make it through what our brain filters out. Along the same line, if you are not making a concerted effort to focus on what you find positive about yourself, you're likely to not think about it. In short, if you aren't recognizing why you're the amazing person you are, while you are continuing to process all those negative stimuli—it's likely you're struggling to love yourself.

I hear people all the time talk about self-love as some kind of "journey." I find this terminology challenging because it implies that loving yourself has a clear trajectory and an endpoint; it doesn't. You don't get in your car of life, follow the right road signs, and end up in love-yourself-land, where you can live out the rest of your life full of self-esteem. Sadly, it doesn't work that way. Someone once described self-care to me as a muscle. If you work at it daily, it becomes stronger and more reliable. As I researched how positive self-perception is manifested in the brain, I found this to be exactly how self-love works. The part of the prefrontal cortex that processes positive self-perception actually swells, just like a muscle, when an individual has a great sense of self-esteem.[34] Mind blown.

By the same token, if you fail to care for yourself the muscle loses power and needs to be rebuilt. The same was seen in scans of the brain: those who have lower self-esteem also had brains that were deflated in this region. If we view self-love as a muscle, we must acknowledge that it takes active practice for it to maintain its strength. In our lives, there will be times when we love ourselves fully and there will be times when we struggle to recognize our own worth. The journey to acceptance is full of peaks and pitfalls. The only thing we can do to best navigate those changes is to be consistent in practices of self-love to keep our positive side of our brand strong.

One of the best ways to build that muscle, and give yourself a self-love boost, is to express gratitude. Living a life full of glitter (a.k.a. positivity) means recognizing the talents, abilities, and support you have been given and acknowledging them in your daily life. In a lot of ways, I find self-love and gratitude to be necessary companions; how can you love something about yourself if you don't first observe it exists?

Often, we are taught to focus on external things we are grateful for, like family, friends, and situational benefits.

However the same practice can be turned inward to recognize things that relate to your personality, behaviors, skills, and achievements. Try keeping a personal gratitude journal where each day you write five things that you are grateful for. For example, my list might include things like fearlessness when talking to strangers, compassion for animals, and the ability to think on my feet. Resist the urge to list things that are not a direct result of who you are. If you are struggling to list things, try to think about times you were kind to others or yourself that day, goals you have achieved, where your practiced good work ethic, your personality, your responsibilities, and any talents. Write down anything you are grateful for, even if it seems small or insignificant. You might think that you should only be grateful for the big things in life, but acknowledging the small blessings is just as important, if not more so. Literally anything that has made your day brighter is worthy of your gratitude and can help you build your positivity muscle.

You'll find by practicing gratitude that you begin to acknowledge and value things about yourself that you perhaps overlooked or didn't feel had worth. Studies have shown that practicing gratitude regularly can reduce depression and increase self-esteem.[35] Additionally, after a while you might find you begin to notice more silver linings in problems you face. Recognizing the silver linings of stressful or traumatic events is a natural result of a more appreciative attitude. When things get really bad, you might find yourself appreciating things you do have more. Gratitude shifts focus our mind toward regular recognition of what we have been blessed with versus living in a perpetual analysis of what we wish we had.

So find a reason to be grateful, flex your self-love muscle. The more you actively recognize how you, the unique person you are, have been gifted with so many amazing skills, talents, and abilities, the better you'll be able to weather storms of negativity and conflict. In future chapters, we'll discuss other ways to build and celebrate just how amazing and worthy you are.

Ways to Build Self-Love

1. Invest in yourself: Self-care isn't selfish; make sure you are making time to take care of yourself so you can avoid unnecessary burnout.

2. Feel all the feels: Express your emotions so you can learn about yourself and improve your interactions with others.

3. Be grateful: Recognize and make time to value the things that make you special.

CHAPTER 5

SELF-COMPASSION: REFRAMING NEGATIVE SELF-TALK

"You alone are enough. You have nothing to prove to anybody."

—Maya Angelou

By the time I was seventeen, I pretty much fully turned my life around. I had gone from getting D's to getting A's in my coursework. I had fundamentally changed the way I saw my capabilities and what I was capable of. I had become less angry and more focused. I was a new Anna.

However, the world didn't see me as such. Although my grades had improved significantly, I was still only a 2.0-GPA student. I worked hard to improve my social skills, but because of my previous behavior those around me were weary to engage with me—let alone trust me to be a friend. Even though I felt like a new person, most people still saw me as the angry, out-of-control deviant teenager I once was. As the world around refused to see what I'd fought so hard to become, I became trapped in a vicious cycle of self-doubt and loneliness. I was hopeless, or so I thought.

Overcoming your past mistakes can be overwhelming. It can feel like each time you try to overcome your past, you are smacked down to the ground with another failure. You might even begin to believe that no matter how much hard work you put in, you cannot change your circumstances. You are destined for a life full of failure, sadness, and night-cheese built on choices made when you were too young to understand how they would affect you. Maybe people can't change. Maybe you should just give up. There's no point in kicking against the pricks, especially when the most painful of those pricks just happen to be yourself.

Even though the voice inside my head was screaming," You can't change. You won't change. You suck. Nobody likes you. You're broken." I somehow mustered up the courage to try one more time. As parts of my brain continued on their very dramatic inner monologue about how I was the worst person ever, totally gross, and not deserving of change, my heart sought to figure out why I felt that way and what I could do to change it. Over time, I recognized that the inner shaming wasn't helping me achieve anything other than keeping me firmly planted where I was.

Why was I so frustrated with myself? I realized it was because felt I had worked really hard and not gotten the results I thought I would. And this is the harsh truth we all must learn—humans are imperfect, and life isn't predictable. Sometimes you do all the right things, in all the right ways, for all the right people and you don't get what you want. You get nothing. Instead of thrashing your dreams of glory, you have to swim past the sea of sameness. Instead of giving up, you have to try something new. Roll the dice again and hope this time all the odds end up in your favor.

What I needed was a fresh start. If those around me weren't going to give me a second chance (their loss), maybe I needed to be surrounded by new people who would give me a chance to make a good first impression. So I did something seemingly crazy. I dropped out of high school, got my GED, and began to research ways to get into college without a formal diploma. I am sure that reading this, you're wondering why I would do something like this.

I must not be thinking clearly. My only argument is that if I had continued doing the same things in the same place, under the same situations, expecting new results—that would be far crazier.

I thought I would end up at community college; I was ready to work my way into a formal university. However my tenacity and this very narrative—my crazy leap of faith to change my circumstances—ended up getting me accepted at a top-100 school. Most college admissions boards have exception committees, a place for students with unusual circumstances to make their case for admission. I definitely was unusual. I explained that learning had transformed my life and that while I was an unconventional student, I had and would continue to fight hard to succeed. I was told that my determination to change and grow were admirable and I was admitted.

This practice of approaching yourself with love, humanity, and mindfulness is called self-compassion. It opened up a world of possibilities for me, and I am confident it can do the same for you. In this chapter we'll address self-compassion and how to use this skill to overcome negative thinking. We'll talk about how we all make mistakes, and how to recognize and adapt your behavior when you are judging yourself too harshly.

AN INTRODUCTION TO SELF-COMPASSION

Imagine your best friend in the world has taken up comedy as a hobby and has recently been taking classes to learn improv. She invites you to see her graduation show for her 101 class, and you go. Watching the show you laugh a little, but it's not perfect. Nor should it be, everyone is obviously still learning. When the show ends, you meet her backstage and tell her how proud you are of her. You tell her how impressed you were that she had the courage to get on stage and put it all out there. You commend her for working hard and learning a new skill. You tell her how much potential you see for her; sure it was a 101 show—but man she made you gut laugh several times. You hug her and tell her you are so glad you got to support her in this new adventure.

Now let's look at another scenario.... Let's say you are trying out a new fitness class for the first time. You show up to class and are the only newbie. Everyone around you has been going for weeks, but you're just starting. You struggle through the workout because it's both hard and unfamiliar. Near the end of class you are exhausted, feel like you're going to throw up, and have to sit out on the rest of the exercises. We've all experienced the mental track that often follows situations like these. You get frustrated. You mull over the fact that you aren't as in shape as the other girls. You think about how stupid you were to even give the class a try. You couldn't even finish it. You're a failure.

When those around us take chances and push themselves out of their comfort zone we cheer them on, but when we ourselves do the same do the same thing, often we can only see our imperfections. Think about how you analyze your performance. It's more than likely, when you analyze yourself, you'll find that you've placed the emphasis solely on the desired outcome. As a result, you tend to see things in black and white—you either achieved the ideal results or you didn't. However, practicing self-compassion, the goal is to see success contextually—you achieved the best you could, given the circumstances by which you entered the situation. When you focus solely on desired outcomes, things like commitment, skill level, circumstances, bravery, etc. are pretty much left unacknowledged. When we analyze ourselves, we tend to set unrealistic expectations and then get frustrated and disappointed when we don't meet them.

However, when we analyze the efforts of someone we love, say your friend pursuing her comedy dreams, we tend to acknowledge context and the potential of the situation instead of the outcome. She's new and she obviously put in the effort to learn, therefore she has done a good job. The context of her experience and effort are the focus versus the outcome (the actual performance). Self-compassion is providing that same loving, fair perspective to how you evaluate your own life. It is the practice of treating yourself—much like you would a good friend—with kindness, humanity, and love.

You also might be wondering how self-compassion differs from self-confidence—aren't they just the same thing with a different name? Self-confidence is a faith in your ability to complete something in the future, while self-compassion focuses on evaluating your current and past choices and circumstances with compassion. Some claim that you choose between the two, but I find that the two are complimentary. Self-compassion is practiced when those hiccups arrive that may send you off course, and self-confidence helps you to face your fears as new opportunities present themselves. Think of self-compassion as your parachute and self-confidence as your jet fuel. Self-compassion, as explained by Kristin Neff, a pioneer in this psychological approach, has three core elements: self-kindness, a belief in a shared human experience, and mindfulness of emotions and actions.

UNDERSTANDING SELF-KINDNESS, HUMANITY, AND MINDFULNESS

As a Type A person, whenever I do a report or a project, it can't just be good. It has to be great. I remember that in college, I pulled an all-nighter finishing the most insane final group project one could imagine. It had charts and graphs and graphs a-plenty. It had insights and action items galore. Strategic insights? I had twenty! But I wanted more.

I worked my fingers to the bone and gave the rest of the group only one assignment—the PowerPoint for our presentation. As I rolled up to meet with my team before class, exhausted and running purely on the adrenaline of the dreams of having the best group project of my life, I got some disturbing news. My team had not made the PowerPoint. Type A me flipped into a set of emotions that I can only imagine would be similar to how one would feel if they had just learned the world was ending the very next day. I spent the next thirty minutes desperately trying to create a presentation on no sleep with out-of-whack emotions. Let's just say the results were...interesting.

As our presentation ended, I could see the disappointed look on our professor's face. I was gutted. I was a failure. Even my best was never going to be good enough. I felt myself spiral into a weird vortex of despair, fueled by a desperate need for a few Z's and my own incessant need to be perfect.

As I sat there, crying over a PowerPoint in the hallway outside class, my professor caught me. "It's just a presentation, Anna. It's not your future. It's nothing more than thirty minutes of your life. Every day, people mess up presentations. It will happen all the time in your career. Get used to it." It's like this teacher had popped into my brain and delivered the exact words I needed to tell myself. I wasn't being very kind to myself, I was overreacting, and she was right; this probably wouldn't be the last presentation that went awry in my life (it definitely wasn't). It wasn't worth blowing up over, it was part of life, and I wasn't very fair to myself.

Self-kindness is the first part of the three cornerstones that make up self-compassion. Practicing this is equivalent to extending love and compassion toward yourself at challenging times. It also means recognizing that failure and struggle are a natural part of human existence. Rather than getting angry, sad, or overwhelmed when life doesn't go according to plan, a person practicing self-kindness approaches the situation logically. These things happen.

There will be times where you work really hard on a report, put every bit of your soul into it, and then forget it on your coffee table when it comes time to turn it in. There will be times when you train all year and sacrifice activities with your friends, only to lose the big race. There will be times when you wake up, look in the mirror, and just don't like what you see back. Self-kindness not only recognizes these experiences, but normalizes them as inevitable parts of our lives. Bad things happen, but practicing self-kindness helps us to rationalize them as a temporary experience or reaction, process them, and move forward.

When my sister died, I distinctly remember sitting in my apartment, feeling terribly alone in my trauma. Why did this happen to me? Why did my sister have to pass away? She had died suddenly of an infarction of her upper intestine; an unusual way to pass. Why did she have to die in a such a weird and unexpected way? She was so young. Why is this happening to me? Why am I so alone in this experience? I am sure you can think of a time in your life when you too had a severe case of "Why me?" It's that gut-wrenching feeling where your brain, heart, and soul collide to scream in unison—"Why is this happening to me and not her or him or them or anyone else? Why me? Why did it have to happen now? Why here? Why me?" It's an agonizing feeling that's not only reserved for when we face extreme traumas. We can feel this pain and loneliness in our emotions during smaller disappointments in life as well. Have you ever been in a class or work setting where you were really challenged and you felt you were the only one making mistakes? Asking "Why me?" is isolating. It makes you feel like you are alone in experiencing disappointing and traumatic events. You are not alone.

When practicing self-compassion to help better endure struggles, you must work to acknowledge them as not being unique to you. In my own personal example, I thought about how I was not the only person that had lost a family member unexpectedly. I was able to find support groups and even counselors that specialized in this type of grief. By recognizing I was not alone, I was able to reach outward for help versus isolating myself in grief. When you reframe life's challenges as a potential shared human experience, you are able to acknowledge that we all feel vulnerable and overwhelmed at times. If all people struggle, we are never truly alone in our experiences. There is always someone, somewhere who knows just how you feel. This not only helps us prevent isolation when life gets dreary, it also increases our support systems, compassion, and understanding of our surrounding community and world.

When I was younger I had the worst temper and my brother loved to torment me to set me off. He'd prod and poke, until I was flipping tables and uttering profanities. It was like a game of Whack-A-Mole for him. Ten dollars to the person who gets Anna to freak out over something ridiculous. I was an over-reactor and was terrible at being mindful of my emotions.

This last part of practicing self-compassion is arguably the most difficult. Mindfulness is an art, and requires us to observe our emotions in a non-judgmental way, which can be really hard in the beginning. By practicing mindfulness, you are literally reprogramming the way information travels through your brain. Research shows that mindful meditation and self-reflection can increase brain composition and processing.[36] Mindfulness also means acknowledging and recognizing when your mind is drawing upon old emotions, and encouraging yourself and your emotional response to return to the present. This allows you to process how you're feeling fairly and make better decisions about how to respond to negative things. Mindfulness increases your general happiness and helps you to overcome the enduring effects of previous traumas in your life.

THE BENEFITS OF A SELF–COMPASSIONATE LIFE

Reading this, I am sure it seems like a lot of hard work. It is. Before I dig into why self-compassion is literally a life-changing approach to dealing with negative self-talk, I want to warn you that it won't be easy. In the beginning, you'll be fighting against years of bad habits and history. Learning to live in the present initially might force you to feel more and may even dredge up a few emotions you haven't truly acknowledged and have been manifesting on other daily events in your life.

There's a saying I came across many times in my research: "When we give ourselves unconditional love, we discover the conditions under which we were unloved." There are reasons you have not been kind to yourself. Many of those reasons are not your fault, but a direct result of the people around you, the way you grew up, and the body/mind you grew into. In order to truly address yourself with the compassion you deserve, you will have to break down the wall around your heart. That way love can enter, and the hurt and disappointment can begin to drain out. Working through those emotions and letting go of your past trauma is painful but incredibly worth it. It won't change overnight, but bit by bit it can become second nature. Living a self-compassionate life reaps amazing long-term benefits that will help you enjoy a happier, healthy, and more positive existence.

A study of students who practiced self-compassion found that they were more likely to be happy, optimistic, and curious. This study also found that these students were also more motivated and took more personal initiative to make changes in their lives. In short, by being kind to yourself you increase your personal potential by first elevating your mood, which allows you to recognize and value more opportunities. This provides you with the strength you need to invest in making the changes you want in your life.[37]v

Not only does self-compassion foster all these positive feelings, it also helps keep you feeling good. Practicing self-compassion leads to what I consider one of the most important things in life—stability. Sometimes stability gets a bad rap. It's not the sexiest thing to talk about. It's boring. However, I think stability is misrepresented; I think stability doesn't have to mean being risk-averse. Stability can also be a firm foundation and perspective which allows you to take better risks with less fear of failure. It helps you think rationally about opportunities, meaning you are less likely to put yourself in situations that would result in unnecessary stress or drama. Self-compassion helps bring a sense of control back into your life. Your emotions and self-esteem begin to stabilize, and you see that same stability extend to other parts of your life. Ditch the chaos and start conquering your dreams.

HOW TO PRACTICE SELF-COMPASSION

Now that I've sold you on the miraculous, life-changing benefits of self-compassion, you're probably itching in your seats for a wee bit of advice on how to actually do it. The first step is to start acknowledging when and where you begin negative self-talk. This sounds easy, but it's trickier than you would think. Most of us are so used to talking to ourselves like we're someone we hate, we aren't shocked enough by the cruel things we say to even register them. One of the tricks I use to help really isolate my inner perspective whenever I am feeling down is to stop what I am doing and think through what's making me feel that way. I continue to ask myself questions until I get to the root negative belief.

Let's say you are getting ready for a hot date. You cycle through 101 potential looks, get frustrated, plop down on your bed, and immediately feel overwhelmed with sadness. Here's how you might question yourself to get to the root negative belief:

Q: Why do I feel sad?

A: I can't seem to find something to wear.

Q: Why is finding something to wear so important?

A: Because I want my hot date to fall madly and deeply in love with me, or at least pay for drinks.

Q: How is not having the right outfit going to prevent you from impressing Mr. Right?

A: Because he won't find me beautiful and interesting.

Q: Why wouldn't he find you beautiful and interesting?

A: Without the right clothes and makeup I'm not attractive.

In this example the root negative belief is uncovered by a series of questions. Once you uncover what is causing you to doubt or think negatively of yourself, you can begin to extend compassion and change how you speak to yourself. Many of us bury emotions to be able to get through when life is cruel. However, moving on from a bout of negative self-talk without addressing the actual reason you're feeling less than chipper is like to trying to fix a toothache with some aspirin. Sure the pain will be relieved temporarily, but you still have a problem that's only going to get worse the longer you ignore or try to bury it.

The gut reaction for someone first starting to actively practice self-compassion is, much like the tooth scenario above, to correct the phrase and ignore it. For example, saying something like, "No, you are beautiful," and then trying to ignore that you ever felt ugly. Unlike other practices, self-compassion first starts with acknowledging the emotion or perception as a normal part of life that many other people have also experienced. You could for example say something like, "I know you are feeling unattractive right now and it's causing you a lot of stress," or " I know you're really excited for this date and are also nervous that they won't find you attractive." It's important that you acknowledge these feelings with empathy and without judgment.

The next step is to acknowledge the actual thing that is bothering you and address why you might feel the way you do. The goal is to focus on your current state and emotions, but remember in the beginning that will be very hard to do. Remember to be compassionate toward yourself as you grow within this practice. Using the example above you might try to say something to yourself like, "I am feeling unattractive today because in previous relationships people have commented on my appearance not being enough and it hurt me. I feel like finding the perfect outfit would take away that fear. I also know it's unfair to assume that this new person will treat me badly. I am anxious because I am letting past interactions and emotions dictate how I live my life."

Once we have acknowledged the root emotion and its triggers, the final step is to assess how you might work toward a better state. It's important to realize you probably won't resolve a deep-rooted negative emotion right away and also acknowledge that you are not alone in feeling the way you do. That's why it's crucial that you always be kind to yourself and realistic in your potential solutions. You might address yourself with something like the following: "We all feel less than perfect sometimes. I am going to make an effort to try and be less critical of my appearance in the future. I am also going to remind myself that my appearance is not the only thing that matters and that there is more to me than how I look. I am going to try harder to acknowledge all the things that make me attractive and not just my physical appearance." In Chapter 4, we talked about how we often treat friends better than we treat ourselves. Self-compassion is working toward extending that same type of kindness to ourselves. If you wouldn't say negative/harmful things to a friend or someone you love, why would you say them to yourself?

These steps take time and lots of practice, so don't be so hard on yourself if in the beginning it seems impossible. Practice and consistency will eventually improve your ability to practice self-compassion by recognizing, addressing, and seeking to resolve negative self-talk. Eventually, you will begin to see the benefits of your effort through more stable emotions, a more positive outlook, and a greater desire to be your best self.

Practicing Self-Compassion

1. Recognize: Acknowledge the root negative self-belief.

2. Address: Face why you believe the negative self-belief to be true.

3. Resolve: Focus on a broader perspective and let go of past trauma.

CHAPTER 6

BULLYING: OVERCOMING BULLIES AND NAYSAYERS

"When they torture me, they show they're weak. When I survive, I show I'm stronger."

—A.S. King

I can still remember how it felt in middle school to be alone. People would chase me down the hall screaming "Kool-Aid Man!" or whatever other terribly uncreative way they had come up with that day to comment on my weight. At lunch they would throw creme-filled sandwich cookies at me, an expensive joke to "feed the beast." The beast was me, a round blonde girl with oversized Coke-bottle glasses and an unhealthy obsession with band T-shirts and khaki-colored polos. In a world where I very much would have rather been able to completely disappear, I was forced to stand out. So that I could be shamed. So that other people could remind me daily why I wasn't worthy or pretty or capable or any of the other things everyone else was.

I am quite certain my middle-school experience was not unique. Maybe while reading the chapter above, your eyes began to swell with big juicy tears, because you too know what it's like to have to endure. Maybe you're going through it right now. Maybe in this moment it's you who feels humiliated and alone. Maybe you don't know what exactly to do.

There was one point where middle-school Anna cracked. I was at lunch when a wild-haired boy, with a devilish grin and even more devilish intentions, hurled a Little Debbie oatmeal cookie (yes, I remember the exact cookie that spawned my reaction) at my face. It made a loud thwapping noise as it cracked against my head, and I heard a table of juvenile boys burst into laughter. I remember taking that very sandwich, and holding it in my hands. I didn't deserve this and I was pissed.

I sauntered over to that very table where the boys were still cackling and congratulating themselves on their hilarious humiliation. I opened the wrapper to the sandwich slowly, as their heads turned to me. Just as deliberately I removed the sweet gooey cookie treat from its plastic cage. I stood directly behind the ringleader of stupidity and I held that sandwich high like a gift from the gods. With all the fearlessness I could muster I brought the sandwich down hard onto his popular head. I mushed that sandwich. I squished it good. I rubbed it into his hair like I was making mashed potatoes. It was a mush-a-palooza. "I am a beast," I uttered, as creme and cookie bits flew everywhere.

I wish I could resolve this story in this moment of triumph of good over evil or, rather, uncool chubby girls over cruel teenage boys, but alas, the story does not end there. I was taken to the principal's office. I was punished. The boys? Well, they weren't punished at all and resumed harassing me with greater vengeance. When you fight fire with fire, nothing gets better; everything just burns to the ground.

Over the next fifteen years, I would try dealing with bullying in every way ever shown in a textbook drama. Anger. Sadness. Tattle tailing. Revenge. You know how it feels, when you are beat down and want your tormentor to be held responsible for their crime. It can become an obsession. They deserve to be punished, and you will tell anyone and everyone until they are. All your energy becomes directed toward bringing them to justice. When we focus on those who try to bring us down or hurt us, we waste energy we need to grow. Bullies win not by humiliating us, but by distracting our attention from what matters in our lives, by preoccupying us with trouble they create in theirs. It might even be said that the easiest way to hurt a bully is to ignore them. Because when you ignore them, you are withholding the one thing they want more than anything—attention.

In this chapter we'll talk about why people resort to bullying and why it's a complicated problem. We'll talk about how to deal with bullying and different methods for coping with abuse. We'll also talk about how to give criticism and feedback without becoming a bully yourself.

WHY PEOPLE BULLY

In an old Buddhist teaching, they tell a story of an unfamiliar dog. If you were to come across a dog and they reared their teeth at you and growled, you'd likely be scared. However if you looked closer and saw that same dog had their own leg caught in a hunter's trap, you might instead feel compassion and understanding for why the dog is behaving as he is. Just like this dog, there is nothing more misunderstood then why people bully others. We are often taught to see bullies as alone in their actions, but often bullies are made from the product of their circumstances, misfortune, and environment.

Have you ever felt out of control? Maybe something traumatic has happened, and normal, everyday things you used to count on are no longer so common. You might feel hurt or upset. You might even feel confused. You'll probably try to do things to make things feel more normal or at least to give yourself a bit more control over the situation. When a person is engaging in bullying behavior, they are often in a similar position—looking for control in their own personal chaos.

When we discuss bullying, we often personify aggressive and malicious behavior as a character trait; a person is a bully. However, this is a learned behavior. A person isn't born a bully, a person has learned to bully. In fact, simply extending this moniker to someone limits their ability to actually change. Research has shown that labeling a student as a bully can prevent them from overcoming negative behavior patterns.[38]

When someone is harassing somebody, they are often purposely choosing an unfair opponent or a person they feel is beneath them for some reason.[39] Then they torment or bother the individual, knowing they are able to hurt them—emotionally or physically. In this way, someone engaging in bullying behavior has control over someone's feelings—which is a satisfying proxy when they are unable to manage their own emotions. Bullying is about control. The oppressor uses power to create an environment where they can control the results and call all the shots. Bullying becomes an alternative reality for the oppressor that, while negative, provides the stability they crave.

Research on shared characteristics for those who bully found that they are likely to have experienced a stressful or traumatic situation in the past five years, and they use bullying as a coping mechanism for dealing with stress. One in three of those who bully people daily said they feel like their parents/guardians don't spend enough time with them. Additionally, they are more likely to feel like those who are closest to them make them do things that they don't feel comfortable doing and aren't very supportive or loving.[40]

The worst part of this research is that most of those who bully do so because they themselves are bullied. Research showed that those who have experienced bullying are twice as likely to go on and bully others. You might think of it this way. A bully is thinking, "If I can't be different and unique without being tormented, neither can you." Much like the "dog in the trap" analogy, those who bully others are hurt and are looking to control and protect their environment in the only way they know how. By being at the top of a perceived power structure, these individuals find a temporary sense of comfort and safety at the cost of the well-being and happiness of those around them. To someone who regularly bullies, this stability and control in their personal chaotic world is essential to their own ability to cope.

This does not justify or imply that bully behavior is acceptable. Instead, I hope it helps you to better understand why people bully others, what their motivations are, and why they might have chosen to bully you. More importantly, I hope you realize that those who bully are the problem, not you. Their behavior isn't a result of something wrong with you, but rather a reflection of something wrong with them that they are not dealing with in a healthy way — simply because they may not know how.

DEALING WITH BULLYING

When someone else is bullying you, the first thing you need to realize is that they have a problem. Their poor behavior is not a result of something that is wrong with you. As we discussed in the previous section, this type of behavior is a coping mechanism and not a reflection of your skills, abilities, or, most importantly, worth. This can be hard to remember — especially when you are bullied by more than one person at once.

Second, it's okay to feel upset. When someone bullies you, they purposely look for things that make you different and exploit them. We talked in previous chapter about how all humans desire to belong. When you are bullied, your oppressor is deliberately exploiting that need by trying to make you feel you are not part of the community. That's a terrible, rotten, no-good feeling. It's the worst. Enduring torment by another human being for something that makes you different isn't easy. You can't just turn off the self-criticism that awakes in you. The most important thing you can do is to acknowledge and react to how you are feeling. It's helpful to actively reflect on who you are as a result of bullying.

Self-reflection is one of the main components of a high Emotional Intelligence or EQ (Emotional Quotient), and it turns out that people with higher EQs are less fazed by bullying. This is because the more in tune you are with your emotions and the cause of them, the more you can make decisions to better your situation. Many will convince you that when bullied, you should put on some type of armor and just pretend that it doesn't suck. The problem with not acknowledging the effect negative words and actions have on you is that you also shut yourself off to other feelings. When we become desensitized to hate, we also become desensitized to love. Acknowledging and recognizing your emotions is important. It is the only way we progress. If we don't feel the hurt, we can't feel the love either. In the moments of doubt and hatred, this is hard to do. However, when you stand up and continue to be who you are without fear, it's then that you become strong. This can only happen if you avoid the temptation to become apathetic and desensitized to the world around you.

Even though you are feeling all these emotions, resist the urge to "fight back." We get taught fairly early that it's a dog-eat-dog world, and that we have to "stand up for ourselves." However it's that same perspective that has created the vicious cycle of bullying that we find ourselves trapped in. We do not fight bullying with bullying. Hate plus hate does not equal love, and it never will.

While addressing abuse with more anger will not improve anyone's circumstances, there is an art to rationally and calmly addressing bad behavior and refusing to accept it. One thing to remember is that someone bullying you wants to control you and, more importantly, your emotions. When they say hurtful things to you, they want you to react. So when you give them anger or sadness, you are giving them what they want. However, when you react calmly and demand respect, you are taking their power by refusing to fall victim to their attempts to hurt you.

I am sure this sounds impossible. This crazy blonde woman wants me to confront the person bullying me with compassion and logic, versus the volcano level anger that I've got brewing inside of me because of their terrible behaviors? If it sounds hard, that's because it is. I am not going to sit here and pretend that confronting your tormentor without using the same vicious, hurtful tactics is easy. However, it is worth it. It's worth it to share your truth. It's powerful to respond without feeding into their need for control. There is nothing more liberating than learning to stand up for yourself without being an asshole in the process.

It saddens me to have to add this, but there will be times in your life where bullying goes above and beyond what any one person should endure. If you see or are the victim of repeated bullying that affects your well-being or places you in danger, make sure you report the incident to someone in charge (a parent, a boss, an HR manager, etc.) or an otherwise authorized individual. In severe cases, you might even need to involve the authorities. You deserve the right to feel safe living your day-to-day life, and anyone whose behavior is threatening that right should be reported.

HOW TO COPE

There are several amazing ways you can cope with bullying—especially if an end to the torment seems eons away. Here are four ways to deal with bullying effectively in your life. These four ways to cope with bullying make up the word D.E.E.L.: disengage, emote, enjoy, love. First, *disengage* yourself from the situation if you can. Second, *emote*—allow yourself to process the feelings associated with the bullying fully. Third, do something you *enjoy*. Lastly, surround yourself with people who know you and love you for who you are. We'll go into each of these coping categories and talk about how they can help you cope with bullying in your day-to-day life.

Disengage

Every once in a while, as an online personality, something I create will go viral and be consumed by far more than my usual audience. The broader the audience that sees my content, the more likely it is for my images to pop in the path of people who don't appreciate them. This leads to hordes of people negatively discussing everything from my weight, to my style choices, to how they perceive my lifestyle—all in a public forum that conveniently notifies me with each little heartless zing. It's great. So when this happens, when the world is talking about me online, I shut off my computer, I turn off my phone, and I separate myself from the chaos. I have learned, by making the wrong choice a million-and-one times, that the easiest way to deal with online hate is to separate yourself from it. I don't Google myself and have mechanisms for filtering out comments that are offensive on my own pages. They can say what they want, but I do not have to indulge them by consuming and reacting to their hate.

Just like the above, perhaps the easiest and most logical way to cope with bullying is to separate yourself from the torment—where possible. Just disengage. Now, this isn't to say you should avoid responsibilities or activities you enjoy in order to curb harassment. Instead, this coping mechanism is best used when you have the power to remove yourself—physically or emotionally—from the situation with little to no opportunity cost. Remember those who bully likely get satisfaction by causing you to react, so by refusing to respond and separating yourself from the situation, you take that power away.

Emote

The second tactic from dealing with bullies is making sure you're fully emoting. We talked earlier about how emotions can be expressed in multiple ways. Often when we are bullied, we try to not react in order to take satisfaction away from our tormentor. However, by not expressing your emotions, you are bottling them up inside yourself. Research has shown that this behavior (suppressing or avoiding your emotions) can actually make them stronger. It's important when you feel overwhelmed or upset to face those emotions head on where you feel safe.

There are a variety of ways you can work through these emotions: journaling, conversations with supportive friends and family members, and meditation are all good approaches to recognizing and reacting to how bullying is affecting your life. Coming up with an action plan on how to deal with similar situations in the future can help give your mind some mental resolution and act as a clear next step in improving your situation. It's important to keep in mind that emotions have three parts to them, and when feeling an emotion, we experience a combination of its mental, physical, and behavioral components. That's why engaging in physical activities such as running, shooting hoops, etc. can also feel fulfilling when we are upset. These activities can help us process the physical components of our emotions, while at the same time releasing endorphins which stabilize and build our mood.

Enjoy

There was a time when I was working professionally and my two bosses were dueling for power. This put me in an unusual situation where on a daily basis I saw bullying as well as experienced it. I was literally between a rock and a hard place. By the end of each workday, I wanted to cry into my pillow and I woke each morning trying to decide if today would be the day I quit. It was unbearable, but I needed to find a way to cope. I knew the situation was temporary. If I could find something to make each day brighter, I could survive. I thought about my favorite places in Austin, where I was living at the time, and one place sprung to mind—Pinballz. It was an old arcade with aisles and aisles of vintage pinball machines. So it started. On rough days, I played pinball. Pinball became my escape and source of joy, when days were hard. It was a world free of the day-to-day stress of my life. I always left with a spring in my step, and sometimes a little taffy I had won in my pocket.

Just like my pinball experience taught me, another way to deal with bullying is to take part in activities that bring you joy. What better way to counteract negative energy than to replace it with positive! Think about simple things you can do in your day-to-day life to boost your mood or increase your confidence. Some examples might include singing, coloring, talking a walk, or cuddling with your dog or cat.

When we find ourselves faced with bullying, it's even more important to make space for some joyous self-care.

Love

If you're going through a rough time, it's important for you to realize you're rarely going through it alone. Bullying can drive us to isolation from shame or embarrassment; however it is then that we most need support and love from those around us. Don't be afraid to reach out to those you love for kind words, encouragement, or advice. Supportive people can help you readjust your self-perception to be more well-rounded and help us shake off any feelings of exclusion or separation. You can use these positive interactions to recharge your batteries and refocus on the opinions that matter most—the ones you have about yourself.

How to "D.E.E.L. with Bullying"

+ Disengage: Remove yourself from the situation where possible.

+ Emote: Share your feelings and process that emotion—don't hold it all in!

+ Enjoy: Do things you enjoy and remember what makes you special.

+ Love: Spend time with friends, family, and others you love.

STOP THE BULLYING CYCLE

As we previously addressed, bullying is a learned behavior that many of us experience too regularly by the time we are teenagers. As a result, we are overexposed to examples of how to critique someone in a demeaning way and are undereducated in how to provide meaningful feedback to help someone grow. As a result, often we approach someone as if we are trying to help them, but actually end up bullying them. We provide criticism on their behavior or work without giving them clear opportunities to improve. This is simply because we don't know how to provide feedback. Bullying is all we've learned.

One of the most powerful skills you can develop in your lifetime is the ability to give someone feedback without attacking them. People who are adept at this skill are not only great mentors, but natural leaders. It makes sense— you're more likely to trust someone who is helping you better yourself. However there is a fine line between helping people around you to grow and develop and manipulating someone else's insecurities to take advantage of them. So how does one provide feedback without stepping into bully territory?

Remember to, whenever possible, start on a positive note, provide specific feedback, and help the individual know the value of applying said feedback. For example, instead of saying, "This report is useless and sloppy," you might say something like, "Thank you so much for working hard on this report. When I read through it, it seemed a bit disorganized. On pages 4–5 your points were unclear, and I wasn't sure what you were trying to convey." In this example we are first acknowledging a positive (the creator's hard work), then giving specific feedback ("pages 4 and 5 are unclear"), and lastly, implying the value in addressing or applying this feedback (that the message will be clearer for readers to understand). Remember, if possible, to try and take the individual out of the critique; you're providing feedback on someone's work, not the person overall. Also, if you are providing feedback but not helping them realize the benefits of making those changes, you're not giving feedback. You're bullying them.

There will be times in your life where you have to critique an aspect of someone's personality. These are the most difficult criticisms to give, because they will always be personal. In these situations it is important to note how the behavior makes you feel in addition to the other feedback points we discussed. For example, "Tim, I like your enthusiasm. That said, however, you're not dependable and I cannot count on you to be an active member of this team. As a result, I don't feel comfortable promoting you." In this example, we're explaining how Tim's lack of dependability makes us feel uncomfortable promoting him. It is important to not state absolutes, because it implies to the receiver that the outcome can't be changed—and a good mentor knows that we can all grow and develop. In short, you can avoid being a bully by making sure every critique you provide to another has a purpose, clear feedback, and a clearly expressed value of making the stated changes.

CHAPTER 7

GOALS: CREATING A CAUSE FOR SELF-CELEBRATION

"The more you praise and celebrate your life, the more there is in life to celebrate."

—Oprah Winfrey

Have you ever had a dream that seemed silly or impossible, but knew in your heart of hearts that you had to achieve it? I remember having a dream where I was running. I was speeding through cornfields, zooming down alleyways, and feeling the wind at my back. In that dream, I felt free. I woke up that morning convinced I was meant to be a runner.

Prior to my hazy revelation, my experience with running was minimal to say the least. I had probably run a total of a quarter-mile in the past six years combined. I could not even remember the last time I ran anywhere; I didn't even own tennis shoes. Despite how ill-equipped I was, I made up for it in spirit. Despite all the reasons why this might be a bad idea, I headed to the shoe store and bought my first pair of running shoes.

What I have always found odd is that when you try to change your habits, so many people rush to tell you that you can't. Fat girls can't run. You're going to injure yourself. You should stick to walking. Perhaps you feel this now. You have the dream, but find that the world around you seems to be trying to stop you from even trying. You expect the world to cheer you on, but often it doesn't.

I started running a minute at a time. Those were the longest minute-intervals of my life. I'd stand hunched over at the end, gasping for breath and praying that I wouldn't die. However, little by little, I got better. I began running farther for longer. I never ran very fast, but I was running—I was doing it. It was a magical day the first time I ran in the sun with the fields at my back. My dream became my reality.

In this chapter, we'll talk about setting goals you can achieve. We'll discuss why your brain fights change, how to fight back, and why celebration is essential to long-term success. I'll introduce you to a strategy you can use to help you focus on the most important goals in your life. If you're looking to make a change, this chapter will give you a head start in doing so.

WHY ACHIEVING YOUR GOALS IS SO DANG HARD

If you haven't yet figured out while reading, I love studying how the brain works. So when I started researching goal setting, I dove right back into my cranium studies and discovered some pretty crazy obstacles that make achieving goals really hard. Way back in Chapter 2, we talked about schemas and how our brain uses them to define and store patterns to process information more quickly. Our brains love a good pattern, and that behavior extends to our actions and reactions to any stimuli. For most scenarios, your brain is leveraging a preexisting schema to help it make a quick decision on how to respond. This means much of the processing is happening lightning-fast and at the subconscious level. You don't even know it's happening.

According to research by M.K. McGovern, a Fellow in psychiatry at Stanford University, habits are simply actions learned in a sequence and performed unconsciously to free up a little brain space for thinking about more important things—like that cute boy who makes your latte at the coffee shop, or where to have brunch with your friends on Saturday.[41] As a result, sometimes we repeat behaviors out of habit, without even giving ourselves time to evaluate why we are doing so. These "autopilot" behaviors can make improving a negative habit quite challenging because you might not even know you are doing it until it's too late.

Additionally, according to research by various neurologists, outlining a goal mentally means it becomes a part of how we define ourselves, as if we've already accomplished it. That means, by setting something as a firm objective, our brain perceives the desired outcome of that goal as a necessary part of who we are. It doesn't matter how large or small the aim—it becomes essential to our identity. In some ways this is good, as it encourages our brain to create scenarios to help us perceive our desired future reality as true. However, there are negatives as well. Once we recognize a goal as essential to our identity, we begin to experience a sense of emotional dissonance if we have not yet achieved it. For example, if I set a goal to be a runner, my mind begins to think of me as a runner, and gets irritated when I am unable to run initially. To my brain, I'm a runner—I should be able to run. It's why often when we try new things we are excited about, but aren't magically great at the first time, we beat ourselves up for it. By setting a goal we have defined it as essential to who we are, leading to emotional distress and even depression when we aren't yet who we feel we need to be.[42] I bet you didn't expect to read about how goals are depressing, but here we are.

Let's go one step further. Sometimes, when we visualize our goals, we actually increase the potential distress our minds might go through. We envision a final fantasy destination, one with perfect results. Unfortunately, that end state doesn't take into account the challenges you might be faced with in order to achieve those results. It also doesn't factor in sacrifices or tradeoffs you might encounter. This can leave you feeling less motivated to achieve your goals when you are faced with roadblocks to success in real life. Jeremy Dean, a psychological researcher at University College London, found that fantasizing about achieving a goal releases some of the same feel-good chemicals as actually achieving it, leaving us less motivated to pursue the actual completion.[43]

IDENTITY VS. OUTCOME-BASED GOAL-SETTING

Often when we set goals, we tie them to an event or milestone we use as a marker of achievement. I want to win the state championship basketball game. I want to lose twenty pounds. I want to run a mile in eight minutes. All of the previous desires are excellent examples of traditional goal setting. The challenge with setting these types of goals is they focus on a specific endpoint or outcome. When a goal has a specific milestone, it is more likely we will fantasize about its completion. As we discussed in the chapter on competition, when we focus and attach our emotions solely to the outcome of an activity, this can take away the joy of doing it. That means we lose all the fun, happiness, and fulfillment derived from the process of taking on new behaviors that cause us to change. This can make the process to change unwilling; let's look at an example.

Let's say you want to be healthier [44] and you set a goal to lose 10 pounds. Over the next few weeks, you will do everything you can to lose poundws—even if you don't enjoy it. Perhaps you eat foods you don't enjoy or, worse yet, don't eat enough at all. You might also exercise excessively; anything, just to make the number on the scale move. When you do finally lose the weight, you might feel proud that you achieved your goal, but it won't necessarily be enough to compensate for all the negatives your body experienced during the process. Therein lies the problem with goals based solely on outcomes. When we focus on a singular milestone, we can lose sight of the progressive behaviors that not only help us achieve our goal but provide more sustained enjoyment overall.

Let's look at another way to set goals. Instead of focusing your efforts on the outcome, focus on what you want to become. Let's say you want to run a 5K. Now, if you were working on outcome-based goal setting, you'd pick a 5K occurring sometime in the future, create actionable steps backward from the race's date, and work day-by-day toward running that race. However, in this example, before making any decisions, first ask yourself why running a 5K is important to you. Is it because you want to be a runner? Or because you want to be healthier? Why are you determined to run that race? That should be where you focus your energy—the core of why you are running.

So let's say you want to be a runner, and you have your hopes set on running a 5K in a few months. You should say to yourself, "I want to be a person who runs regularly and competes in races." This is an example of setting an identity-based goal. Here you are mentally committing to a change in how you identify yourself through your efforts. In this way, you are preparing your mind to alter the schema that fundamentally defines who you are. Each and every run then becomes proof that your schema should adapt to this new identity.

Rather than accepting your new identity (a runner) only once you achieve a goal (for example, complete a 5K), you are training your mind to recognize this identity immediately as a real reflection of who you are. Think of this like a mental game of faking it until you make it. In this way, you aren't just achieving a goal, but rather are affirming a self-proclaimed change in who you are repeatedly. This forces your brain to evaluate yourself and your behaviors differently, over time altering your subconscious behaviors to match your evolved identity. In simpler terms, if you keep telling yourself you're a runner and force yourself to do things runners do, then eventually you will believe you are a runner and naturally want to do those things.

Using identity-based goals doesn't mean that outcome-based goals are worthless. Instead, a combination of the two is likely most effective. Outcome-based goals are your macro goals and help you acknowledge major achievements. Identity-based goals are your micro goals and help you manage change and establish small wins that act as motivators as you develop new habits. Using a mixture of identity- and outcome-based goals together can work to keep us motivated and focused, and help us consistently recognize progress.

> **Identity vs. Outcome Goals**
>
> 1. Identity Goals: Goals based on who we are and who we want to become.
>
> 2. Outcome Goals: Goals based on what we want to achieve.

HOW TO SET GOALS

I am going to start this section saying something totally crazy, but probably true. You have too many goals.

I bet you have goals you want to achieve at work. There's probably some goals you have for your future. Maybe you have some goals for your love life. Oh, I bet you also have goals for personal development. You might have goals for your neighborhood. Goals for your dog. Goals on goals on goals. In fact, I am going to guess that the biggest thing getting in the way of you achieving any of these goals is that you simply have too many of them. Your goals are getting in the way of you achieving your goals. It sounds ridiculous, but it's the truth.

Let's say you're in your car driving down a highway. On a fifteen-minute trip you'll probably pass fifteen to fifty advertisements, depending on where you live. How many of them can you remember? One, maybe two—if any at all. This is how our brain reacts when we create too many goals. It begins to just ignore them altogether. Your mind simply can't focus on one thing long enough to progress when it has eighty-five other things pulling at your focus on a daily basis. You might achieve something, but just which something is kind of left to chance. Worse, you might achieve nothing—other than detailing a lovely list of goals you'll never achieve.

How many times have we heard phrases like this: "I was supposed to go to the gym today—I'm trying to go every other day, but it's okay because I spent more time with Alex, which was another one of my goals." Or: "I was totally supposed to work on that paper, but I was really focused on having a conversation with Sarah and I'm really trying to value my friendships more. So, even though I totally blew off that important paper, it's ok." Lots of goals also mean lots of reason to celebrate, and plenty of reasons sweep the things we aren't progressing on under the table. We allow ourselves to take one step backward on one goal, in order to celebrate a small step forward on another. In this way, we stay stagnant because we never actually devote enough time to make real change in our life and just sort of ping-pong backward and forward based on what we choose to do daily. Candidly, with this behavior you're not setting goals at all, you're just giving yourself reason to feel better about the choices you make.

Like so many things in life, when it comes to setting real, achievable goals, less is more. Your brain is going to do everything it can to speed up processing and simplifying tasks, so it's in your best interest to keep it simple. Reduce your goals to concentrate on specific areas of focus, and then actually give yourself the mental capacity to achieve them. As a bonus, by limiting your goals to a meaningful few, you also remove much of the unnecessary guilt that comes from rampant unfilled goal-collecting. Research by Edwin Locke and Gary Latham found that setting specific goals which are also challenging is essential to success and leads to higher performance 90 percent of the time.[45] Any goal you set should push your limits and be clear and concise—make it easy for your brain to understand, digest, and implement it.

EXERCISE: SHORT-, MEDIUM-, AND LONG-TERM GOALS

I like to manage goals using a ten-step methodology, broken up as "3-3-3-1." In this exercise, you set ten goals that are aligned to improving your happiness in the short-, medium-, and long-term. Let's say you are trying to get a promotion at work and to date more. We'll use this as an example of how to set these goals throughout this exercise.

Short-Term Goals

Your first three goals are things you are already working toward and hope to accomplish in the next two to four months. These goals are important because they take into account things you are already working on and foresee as achievable. They also create a near-future opportunity to celebrate your progress. Research has shown that celebrating actions and progress toward our goals regularly is critical to our success. When we show progress our brain releases dopamine, giving a satiated feeling that can help us positively condition new behaviors. When we fail to acknowledge our achievements and don't celebrate them, we also fail to acknowledge our hard work and the sacrifices we have made for those achievements. This can cause the rush of achievement to be reduced and cause us to lose focus on achieving long-term goals. Using the example above, your short-term goals might be to put yourself on some dating sites (hello, Tinder!), take a class to build your communication skills (good for work and love), and find three opportunities to promote your achievements to senior employees at work.

Medium-Term Goals

The next set of three goals are your medium-term goals or things you feel you should be able to accomplish in the next four to eight months. You may not be certain how you plan to achieve them, but you are confident you can. You recognize them as achievable, but perhaps a bit beyond your current day-to-day plans or skills. These goals will take some change in your life, but nothing that feels overwhelming or unfeasible. In this example, your medium-term goals might be to go on ten dates, lead and complete a project at work, and make a plan for your ideal career next step.

Long-Term Goals

The last trio of goals are your long-term goals, the ones that involve major change in your life and seem the furthest away from accomplishment. These are goals you're hoping to achieve over the next year. You'll need the success of the short- and medium-term goals to help you emotionally and physically achieve these loftier, meatier goals. To continue with our example, your long-term goals could be moving to a more senior-level job, being in a committed relationship, and learning how to balance work and personal life.

DREAMING BIG

When I was eight years old, someone asked me what I wanted to be when I grew up. A precocious child, I remember turning around, looking them square in the eye and responding, "I want to be a renaissance woman." That desire has stuck with me since then, and has served as my grand goal of sorts. Desiring that renaissance woman lifestyle in my mind, I've taken risks I might not have taken otherwise. I've learned languages, lived abroad, took chances in my career, and always kept learning. Now some twenty-five years later, I'm an author, marketeer, speaker, fashionista, scientist, analyst, and more. That grand goal I set as a child became a lens through which to see my future differently and allowed me to continually learn and reinvent myself.

Just like becoming a renaissance woman, some goals can't be achieved in a year or two—some goals require a lifetime of focus. Strive to set one life goal with the knowledge that it can't and won't be achieved in a year's time. However, acknowledging you want something in your life now will help you make the right decisions to ensure you achieve that goal sometime in the future—even if it takes years. Additionally, if you adapt to take on the identity associated with the desired outcome, you'll make better choices to get you started on your journey to becoming just that.

A Ten-Step Approach to Goal Setting

✦ 3 Short-term goals: accomplished in two to four months

✦ 3 Medium-term goals: accomplished in four to eight months

✦ 3 Long-term goals: accomplished in eight months to two years

✦ 1 Lifetime goal: accomplished across several years

HOW TO ACHIEVE YOUR GOALS

Now that you've set some awesome goals that are clear and actionable, and which appeal to both your identity and desired outcomes, all you have to do is achieve them. About 92 percent of people fail to achieve their annual goals, so let's talk about how you can be part of the 8 percent that do.[46] First and foremost, write your goals down. People who write their goals down have been shown time and time again to be more likely to complete them. According to recent research by Dr. Gail Matthews, a psychology professor at the Dominican University in California, you become 42 percent more likely to achieve your goals and dreams, simply by writing them down regularly. Writing down your goals forces your brain to recognize them both logically and creatively, cementing them in your subconscious.

Let's take this activity one step further. Each week, write down how you plan to work toward achieving these written goals. Making time to recognize and acknowledge what you need to do to attain a goal is an important step toward achieving it. Most goals are actually composed of a hundred or so actions we must take before we can produce the result we want. To go back to our previous example, I can't run a 5K if I don't buy running shoes, stretch, and practice regularly. I need to complete exercises every week, reaching months in the future, to be able to achieve my goal. Taking time each week to acknowledge our progress and reassess keeps us devoted and aware of our goals. Writing down the actions we need to take allows us to recommit our attention and physical energy toward achieving what we want most.

Let's say you have a new, soft, adorable puppy and you want to teach him how to sit. Every time he sits you'll likely cheer the fluffball on, give him lots of affection, and maybe even reward him with a treat. The puppy then learns that sitting when you ask makes you happy, and when you are happy he is more likely to be rewarded. This not only helps him achieve the initial task (learning to sit on command), but will also help him achieve future tasks because he is conditioned that good behavior is rewarded. Now all the pup needs to do is engage in more and more good actions, if he wants to maximize his affection and treat intake.

We are like the puppy above—the more we reward and celebrate progress toward our goals, the more fun and desirable our brain will see that behavior as being. Therefore, it's important that as we progress toward achieving our goals, we celebrate as much as possible along the way. Every step forward needs a resounding cheer. These moments help your body and mind recognize joy and pride in association with the new behaviors.

I remember working with a young intern named Sarah when I was a manager at a software company. She was brilliant and desperately wanted to work for us, but the company wasn't hiring. So we put the power of effective planning to work, and every week we would sit down with our goals in mind and discuss two questions: "What do you think you can uniquely do to help this company? And how are you going to prove that?" Every time I met with her, we would brainstorm ideas to help her achieve in this context.

Every time Sarah took a step forward, we celebrated and I encouraged her to write it down in a spreadsheet or a notebook. Additionally, I helped others celebrate with her by sharing her success with other managers and employees. Often a barrier to our own long-term success is not acknowledging and sharing with others when we have in fact made progress. When review time came around, Sarah had a documented list of the things she'd done, she had a meaningful list of ways she'd helped the company, and she had a bevy of people who knew her for her work ethic and results. At a time when the company was on a hiring freeze, Sarah got a job.

Keeping track of your progress is an essential part of achieving your goals. Oftentimes, we hit a few bumps in the road and quickly forget how far we've come. We instantly see ourselves as failures on the brink of giving up. By keeping track of your little wins along the journey, you create moments to look back on and you can take the time to reflect on the successes you've had up to that point. Reflect on what has worked, and perhaps try to understand what took you off course. You might find, as I often do, that you're being too hard on yourself. A little reflective thinking will have you valuing the progress you've made and have you moving forward again in no time.

CHAPTER 8

LONELINESS: WHAT TO DO WHEN YOU FEEL ALONE

"It is strange to be known so universally and yet to be so lonely."

—Albert Einstein

I was the child of two athlete siblings. My sister was a nationally ranked track star and my brother was a former national champion wrestler. Me, I was a fairly normal, unaccomplished eleven-year-old and as a result, was often forgotten. We spent our weekends shuffling from one practice to another. Many of my childhood memories are of climbing mounds of rolled-up, beat-up and discarded wrestling mats in gyms peppered throughout the Ohio Valley and wandering strangers' school hallways on the weekends. Occasionally, there would be a few other straggler younger siblings to adventure with, but most of the time it was just me.

We all have times in our lives where we feel like supporting actors in someone else's movie. It can feel pointless, boring, and worst of all—lonely. Some of the most traumatic times in your life are not because you feel overwhelmed or devastated, but because you feel isolated, forgotten, and alone. I remember that feeling so much as a child. I would sit behind a stack of mats, wondering how long it would take someone to even notice I was gone. Most the time, not until the night was done. I often felt like a responsibility versus someone people wanted around. That's what loneliness can do. Whether a product of our environment or self-inflicted, feeling isolated from the world around you can make you feel as if your own flaws have somehow made you socially untouchable. Loneliness is one of life's most painful challenges and can make us feel helpless in our own journey.

I remember being particularly distraught one evening and so I started to brainstorm ideas to get attention. My first impulse was to throw a fit. I was eleven, give me a break. It seemed rational to my baby brain. However I quickly learned that no one cared about my theatrics for much more than a few passing minutes. There were more important things to tend to; wrestling was pretty much a sport of the gods where I grew up, and I was merely a roadblock to the necessary worship hour. Defeated, I sat cross-legged on the floor—bored, lonely, and annoyed. I played with my shoelace and watched curiously as a high school girl attempted to sell a saccharine sweet sucker to forty-year old man in an embossed polo. She was struggling.

I have no idea what possessed me to jump in and help, but next thing I knew I was standing beside this teenager, helping her sell this man on the joys of a two-dollar lollipop. I wasn't just good at it. I was great. "You can use it as a top, you can hit your kid with it, you can sing into it like a microphone." I sold this sucker like it was some type of miracle product certain to solve all of life's problems, cure all ills, and somehow make you a hundred dollars in the process. Begrudgingly, the man caved. He had bought a sucker and I had sold my way out of loneliness.

Mat Maids (don't even get me started about the name) was a group of girls in my high school who helped run wrestling events, cheered on the boys, and sold suckers to fund it all. While I was barely in middle school, my candy-pushing abilities soon led them to adopt me into their fold. What I learned from this experience is that the hardest part of loneliness is that 90 percent of the time only you can make it better. You have to take the first step.

A lot of people think that feeling less lonely is as simple as surrounding yourself with others. It's not. We have all been in situations where we have been surrounded by people and yet feel isolated and alone. In this chapter we're going to discuss loneliness—what causes it and how it affects you. We'll also talk about ways to embrace and build your relationships to help you feel less lonely in your day-to-day life.

THREE TYPES OF LONELINESS

Loneliness is one of those emotions that creeps up on you. One day you're minding your business, having a perfectly normal, active social life and—BLAMMO! Suddenly you feel alone. It's like night and day. You might even feel most alone after a big event. It doesn't seem logical; how can you feel by yourself with such a large group of friends and a full life? Well, because everything we've been taught about loneliness is a lie.

Loneliness isn't just felt by the awkward high school teenager who eats alone or the old woman whose partner has just passed, loneliness happens to everyone. It can happen when your life is going great. It can happen when you are surrounded by friends. Loneliness is not a reflection of the number of social engagements you attend or the number of friends you have. The emotion is relative. Dr. Julianne Holt-Lunstad, a woman researching how loneliness affects our health, described loneliness as "the subjective perception of isolation—the discrepancy between one's desired and actual level of social connection."[47] Basically, at a high level, if your current relationships aren't as vast or as deep as you have mentally decided you need them to be, you're going to begin to feel lonely.

It's also important to note that loneliness is not the same as depression. That assumption is another great example of how misunderstood the subject is. You can experience regular, even chronic loneliness without ever being depressed or suicidal. In fact, many people ignore their isolation and how it affects their lives because they don't have those clear feelings of unhappiness to justify getting help. A 2012 study by Dr. Carla Perissinotto at the University of California in San Francisco actually found that the loneliest individuals are married, live with others, and are not clinically depressed.[48]

There are three types of loneliness: situational, developmental, and internal loneliness,[49] and understanding which is causing you to feel lonely can be immensely helpful in combating the negative effects. The first type of loneliness is situational loneliness. This type of loneliness is a result of things that happened in your environment that alter how you perceive your existing relationships. Have you ever had a good friend move away and then feel lonely because they are physically not as available? This is an example of situational loneliness. Your environment has changed. While you still might talk to your friend on the phone regularly, the depth of the relationship probably feels shallower because you can no longer rely on that friend for regular face-to-face interaction. Examples of other things that might trigger this type of loneliness are arguments with friends, accidents, disasters, and loss. Really, anything that happens in your environment that causes there to be a perceived loss in the depth and amount of interactions you have with others.

The second type of loneliness, developmental loneliness, is a feeling of isolation that happens when the balance between the time needed to develop yourself as a unique person (a.k.a. "me time") and the time needed for social interaction is off-kilter. Let's say you take a new job and feel immediately overwhelmed by your new responsibilities. You start working extra hours to get up to speed more quickly. As a result, you have less time to see others and begin to feel lonely. This is an example of developmental loneliness. This can happen because you are lacking certain skills/abilities, find yourself in a new environment, or as a result of extended separations. It can also stem from poverty, marginalization, and status. Luckily, developmental loneliness is usually temporary and resolves itself once your interpersonal relationships are back in balance.

The last type of loneliness is internal loneliness. Internal loneliness is a result of several things: inability to connect with others as a child, mental illness, or poor coping skills. For these individuals, they perceive themselves to be alone, although that may or may not be the case.[50] Unresolved internal loneliness can cause us to feel disconnected from our surroundings, and alone even in the presence of others. Unlike the other forms of loneliness, interpersonal loneliness is more pervasive and self-perpetuating. Many doctors even consider it a chronic illness. It is the learned belief that you are socially inept, unable to connect with others, or naturally unlikable.[51] If not managed, it can lead to feelings of being completely alone in the world, inability to assert oneself, and, in the worst cases, suicidal tendencies.

Throughout my life, I would have odd moments where I would suddenly feel lonely without a clear specific cause. Maybe I'd see a post of a few distant friends together and wonder why I hadn't been invited. Maybe I'd have a really crazy work week and forget to plan anything for the weekend and then be too overwhelmed or scared to ask somebody to hang out. Some days I didn't have anything I could blame, I just felt lonely.

I live with internal loneliness, and learning this has been critical in managing my own happiness. Social media can be a huge trigger of these feelings for me; FOMO (fear of missing out) means much more to a person with internal loneliness. It can trigger feelings of planned exclusion—as if people deliberately sought to exclude you. If you suffered neglect and abuse or were repeatedly excluded because you were different growing up, you might suffer from this type of loneliness.

Three Surprising Facts about Loneliness

✦ You can feel lonely when you are surrounded by people. Loneliness is feeling alone, not the result of being alone.

✦ Loneliness and depression are not the same thing. You can be lonely and not sad.

✦ Loneliness can be a chronic condition that needs to be regularly managed like any other illness.

EFFECTS OF LONELINESS

When we think about people suffering from loneliness, we usually get the picture of an older individual sitting home alone waiting for someone, anyone to call. This is when we've been taught isolation is the worst, when you're older. However this stereotype isn't entirely true. Holt-Lunstad and her colleagues analyzed seventy studies encompassing over 3.4 million people, and found that loneliness peaks in adolescence and in young adults, then again in the eldest in society. According to Louise Hawkley, senior research scientist at the National Opinion Research Centre at the University of Chicago, "if anything, the intensity of loneliness decreases from young adulthood through middle age and doesn't become intense again until the oldest old age." Loneliness is more likely to affect someone under the age of sixty-five than over it. That means you, regardless of your age, could very likely be that person eagerly waiting by the phone for someone to call.

When you feel lonely, your body begins to react. You might feel a bit ill. You might find you have a more persistent cough. It might be harder to breathe. People who have reported feeling lonely have shown to be more likely to experience stronger symptoms when sick and have poorer overall health.[52] And beyond just general malaise, being lonely can break your heart—literally. Research has shown that loneliness is linked to increased cardiovascular risks.[53] When you suffer from prolonged feelings of isolation, your body begins to break down to send a message to your brain—you need help from your community.

They say it takes a village to raise a child. It also can be said it takes a village to raise your overall health. Your body's reaction to perceived isolation is the natural way of pushing you to find a social group. Its instinct is playing its part to save you. Prior to zip-up fleeces and self-driving cars, community was a requirement for survival. You needed others for protection and reproduction. While society might have progressed since those early days, the instincts remain. Humans crave communities and when you feel removed from one—you feel literally sick until you find your tribe.

However finding your tribe may not be so easy. Loneliness can be self-perpetuating. Sometimes when you feel separated from others, you make decisions that prevent you from connecting. For example, if you don't see your friends for a few weeks and then go out to lunch with them, you might find they have a hilarious inside joke you don't understand. Instead of asking for the backstory, if you're feeling lonely you might further isolate yourself. You might even begin to feel like an observer in the experience versus a participant. This is an example of how loneliness can hinder our ability to understand social interactions, resulting in feelings of alienation.

The worst part is that these feelings can escalate. Prolonged loneliness can trigger what psychologists call a "hypervigilance for social threat."[54] This is just a fancy way of saying that when you are lonely you begin to see the world and your experiences in an increasingly negative way. Have you ever felt alone and as a result began to notice all the ways you weren't included in your friends' lives? You might dredge up memories of not being invited to birthday parties or weddings. You might even begin to think the worst of the relationships you do have—assuming people are choosing not to hang out with you rather than just being busy themselves. This perspective isn't limited to our friends, you even begin to see encounters with complete strangers as not only unfulfilling but deliberately negative.

Loneliness has such an effect on our mental and physical well-being that many doctors consider it a modern epidemic. Not only are more and more people feeling lonely, but the copious amount of research done on loneliness shows that this social isolation is just as severe a risk factor as high blood pressure, lack of exercise, or smoking for illness and early death.[55] Doctors, like Richard Lang, chair of preventive medicine at the Cleveland Clinic, are encouraging people to manage loneliness in "the same way they would their diet, exercise, or how much sleep they get."[56] In short, balancing your social connectedness and reducing feelings of isolation in your life is a difficult but important requirement in improving your overall well-being.

YOU ARE PART OF THE PROBLEM AND THE SOLUTION

If you are experiencing loneliness, you are not alone. In the last thirty years loneliness has more doubled; 40 percent of Americans report feeling lonely. And chronic loneliness? It's more common than depression! Ten percent of the population now fights feelings of isolation daily due to chronic internal loneliness.[57] Right now, this very second, across the world, millions of other people are also feeling isolated and unconnected. Being lonely is normal.

Earlier in this chapter, we talked about the different types of loneliness; working to understand what's causing you to be lonely is a great first step to overcoming its effects on your life. You might even find you need external support to help you discover and process why you feel isolated. Once you are able to recognize why you feel alone, you have to acknowledge that emotion. Oftentimes there is a fear that confessing these feelings is weak or wrong. Instead, the opposite is true. It takes a strong person to admit that they are upset about their relationships. It takes an even stronger person to work toward resolving those feelings of desolation.

Once you have acknowledged your own loneliness, examine how your decisions may or may not be contributing to the continuation of your feelings. When you feel particularly disconnected, you might feel exacerbated by everyday activities. No, you don't want to go to book group. No, you don't want to attend Mary's combination bridal shower and craft party. No, you don't want to go to the grocery store, soccer practice, or the mall. The only thing you want to do is complain about how doing anything that puts you around other people will only leave you upset, unfilled, and tired. As a result, you end up just staying home. Feeling like you are on an island by yourself, the loneliness just gets worse and worse.

As we talked about previously, isolation can be self-perpetuating, so you have to take ownership of the emotion and responsibility for your part of the experience. Sure, usually the thing that first triggers us is a valid reason to feel lonely. However, if you find yourself in a cycle of feeling disconnected, it's time to look inward. The reason loneliness is hard to overcome is because it's so much more comfortable to assume other people's problems or oversights are the reason you are alone. It hurts to reflect inward and question the choices you are making that may be causing you to disconnect from others. It's also painful. The root of loneliness is often that nagging subconscious fear that you might be undesirable, unworthy, and completely unlovable. If you try and you fail, you might just prove these painful thoughts to be true.

However, these thoughts aren't true. You are worthy. You are lovable. You have value. This fear is a product of your trauma, a scar from your past pain. Do not let that pain and isolation control your life. Accept that they exist and you will have the power to overcome them. See their effect on your life and refuse to allow them to continue to prevent you from seeing that you are lovable, deserving of healthy relationships, and worthy of human affection.

HOW TO FEEL LESS LONELY

Each and every one of us has someone who loves us and values who we are. We may not know it, but it's true. That's why it's essential, when lonely, to resist the urge to isolate yourself. The days you have the hardest time leaving your home to be around people, are often the days you most need to be. I can reflect back to many times in my life where I would look all day at an event on my calendar with dread. I didn't have the energy to go. However, whenever I pushed myself to show up, I have benefited. When I've stayed home, maybe nothing changed, but certainly nothing got better.

When I am feeling particularly lonely, I force myself to send text messages to five different people whose relationships I value or that I want to get to know better. Usually, regardless of the day, one of those five people is near their phone. This small step toward connection can be a positive step toward bigger social experiences that seem overwhelming. Taking opportunities to create small moments of interaction with others—like a text or a phone call or even a hello on the street to a strangers—can help you mentally rewrite how you perceive yourself.

Maybe you feel alone because you feel like you don't have anyone in your life to connect with or that your current relationships are unfulfilling. In these instances, you need to create new opportunities for relationships to form. The easiest way to create possibilities to meet and get to know new people is to explore a new hobby, take a class, or join a club. You can meet new people who don't have any preconceived opinions of who you are. That can be so incredibly liberating. Additionally, having a planned time for interaction can be helpful by allowing you time to prepare for the experience and ensuring you have time to work on connecting with others. Plus, you get the added bonus of a natural discussion topic. That means that if you're uncomfortable driving conversation about yourself initially, you can talk about the hobby or subject you are learning about. Talking about something you love or that interests you with someone else who also shares that passion is potentially the easiest conversation to have.

If you're struggling to find a hobby or skill you want to explore or can't make time for planned, regular interaction, try supporting people that naturally come into your life on a day-to-day basis. Not only is nurturing others an excellent way to foster and build the deeper, more rewarding relationships we crave, but it also causes physiological changes in the brain that promote happiness. Even little things, like offering a stranger your seat on the bus, can help you feel less lonely and more connected to your community. One thing I do is smile at strangers and stop to pet their dogs when I go for runs. This is an easy and fun way to add a small amount of social interaction into my daily life. Plus, who doesn't love an excuse to pet all the dogs?

Volunteering is another great option to help us combat feelings of loneliness. Working together with others toward a united altruistic goal can help us instantly feel connected. Additionally, volunteering provides a concrete memory of where your hard work has made a difference in the world. This can be drawn upon when loneliness cause you to question your need or value to others.

If you find yourself trying again and again to resolve your feelings of loneliness and you're not seeing any progress, seek professional help. Socially, we are trained to see mental health professionals as people you see when you are sad or self-destructive. This can feel confusing to someone who suffers from loneliness, but not depression. However, mental health professionals are essential in helping some individuals overcome loneliness-especially when that loneliness is internalized.

How to Deal with Loneliness

1. Avoid self-imposed isolation.

2. Explore a new hobby or interest.

3. Nurture existing relationships.

4. Volunteer in your community.

5. Seek professional help and support.

CHAPTER 9

BODY: LOVING THE SKIN YOU'RE IN

"To lose confidence in one's body is to lose confidence in oneself."

—Simone de Beauvoir

I was eleven when I first remember someone explaining to me that my body was something to be ashamed of. We were on vacation and visiting my grandparents in their sunny, golf-cart-fueled senior citizen society just outside Orlando. I was in the kitchen, helping my grandmother prepare a list of items we would need from the store while in Florida.

"Strawberry toaster strudel." I said with a big, cheeky grin. I hadn't visited my grandparents much before, but I knew from TV that if someone was going to let me eat fruit-flavored sugar wrapped in buttery faux pastry and topped with frosting for breakfast, it was going to be my grandma. Grandparents are always the ones baking cookies, prying candies from their lint-covered pockets, and playing innocent after sneaking contraband to their doting grandchildren.

"You don't need that," was my grandmother's stern reply. "But *whyyyyy*," I asked, with my preteen dramatics kicking in. She turned to me and said, "You could stand to lose some weight—nobody likes an overweight girl." I looked her square in the eye, crossed my arms, and said defiantly, "God loves me just the way I am!" She paused, looked away, and with a slight smirk spoke five words I will never forget: "God doesn't love fat girls."

It's likely you too have someone who has made comments about your body that have left you feeling frustrated. In today's world, it is impossible to avoid commentary about our physiques. The ideal standard is everywhere, and our failure to reach the increasingly impossible ideals is rubbed into our faces and minds daily. "Your thighs are too big. Your skin is too blotchy. Your complexion is too dark. Your looks are too different. You should wear more makeup. You should exercise. You should stay out of the sun. You should take better care of yourself." It's as if by not existing perfectly, it is assumed you don't care about yourself at all. Because if you did care, you'd conform.

As a child, I resented my grandmother. As an adult, I realize her actions were just the product of years and years of societal pressures that convince us that maintaining a certain body type is more important than anything else. More important than your happiness. More important than your health. More important than your sanity. Many of us feel conflicting emotions around the choices we make about our form on a daily basis. We've lost touch with our bodies and how using them makes us feel.

You probably know perceptions and expectations of your body are unrealistic, but feel challenged on how to make peace with the skin you're in. How do you separate what you really want for your body from what you feel subconsciously pressured to want? In this chapter, we'll talk about finding that peace. We'll talk about recognizing your body as the amazing support system it is, harnessing the power of meaningful movement, and learning how to make decisions to better your body on your own terms.

BODY AWARENESS VERSUS BODY LOVE

Today's world is littered with conflicting messages about your body. If you open a magazine, on one side of the page, you might see an article about how to learn to love your imperfections, juxtaposed with a glossy ad selling cream to hide your wrinkles on the other side. Open up social media and you'll see celebrities writing inspiring comments about learning to love themselves, followed by a push for you to buy "this super yummy tea that will totally flatten out your stomach." The world constantly talks about how important self-care is, but the actual act of practicing it gets boiled down to ways to fix your body. Masks to make our face better. Diets to make your body sleeker. Treatments to solve problems you didn't even know were problems until the world told you they were. The message has become love the skin you're in, by changing it.

I remember reading an article about cankles in a magazine when I was younger. For those of you who are lucky enough to not yet know what cankles are, it's when your calf and your lower leg appear as one continuous body part. Thus we get "cankles," the fun and insulting combination of the words "calves" and "ankles." In this article,[58] a woman detailed why she chose to cosmetically alter her ankles because of all the ways she felt they were holding her back. Vacations were ruined. Photos were avoided. Shame was endured. I remember reading this splashy glamour magazine piece, convinced that being the cankle queen and having unidentifiable calf muscles was a punishment worse than death. There was only one conclusion: cut my hair, maul my face, but please don't give me cankles.

The trouble was, I didn't really know what cankles looked like. I found myself scouring pictures of ankles online, trying to determine whether they were cursed lower appendages or blessed ones. I looked at my own legs. Were they cankle-ous? I couldn't tell. I found myself stopping coworkers, friends, and even strangers to try and get a clear grasp on my current ankle status.

Turns out cankles were invented as a body concern from a one line said by Jason Alexander in the 2011 movie *Shallow Hal*. Quickly, the press jumped in to save us from this supposedly age-old scourge that was actually created by an offhand comment from a supporting character in a moderately successful, but quickly forgotten movie. It's an excellent example that as fast as we learn to love something about ourselves, the media invents something new for us to hate. How many things about your body do you punish yourself for on a daily basis that only exist as a concern because someone somewhere decided they could profit off of making you feel pain?

Many people will tell you to do more to love your body. I am, unfortunately, not one of those people. Over the years, there has been an increasing trend to isolate the body in one's journey to self-acceptance. However, that trend, in response, has resulted in an unusual overcorrection. The discussion about our bodies is now dominated by accepting perceived flaws or limitations. I love myself even though I have rolls, or freckles, or bad skin, or nappy hair or, yes, even cankles. However, as positive as this trend may seem, it is problematic in it's own way as well.

These conversations focus on appearance—what your body looks like—and they all too often neglect what your body is capable of, how it supports you, and what difference living in it means to your unique existence. In attempting to counterbalance negative body perceptions, we have put our bodies on an island and lost the fundamental connection between how we move and how we exist. We've forgotten that comfort in your body doesn't come from just loving your marketed imperfections, it is found in knowing how your body makes you who you are. It's not about loving your body, it's about loving yourself and including your body as part of that definition.

Building a healthier and more productive relationship with your body starts with improving your physical and sensory awareness. Body sense is the ability to be present in our bodies, feeling our sensations, emotions, and movements in the current moment, without succumbing to judgmental thoughts.[59] It is the link between your mind and your body. In this way, when you have embodied self-awareness, you experience things more fully and are more aware of your physical needs.

The last time you went to the gym, did you like so many others just pop on your headphones and zone out? For years, movement has been pitched to us as a way to disconnect from the world and our thoughts. Maybe, like many of us, you use exercise as a way to mentally check out. Much of our education about mental and physical health treats the two as separate entities. We occasionally hear about how if you work out, the endorphins will make you happier or that if you find ways to be less stressed, you'll want to do more. However, in this scenario, the body and mind are simply two individual things, where one entity is affecting the other. What if you approached the body and mind as single entity? "You."

Body sense is taking in how your body feels in reaction to your emotions and experiences, along with recognizing how physical experiences affect your present mental state. Although this is a relatively new field of study, there is already research that shows body sense can lower your stress, activate your nervous system, and kickstart your immune system. It makes sense. If you listen to and experience more things through your body, you're bound to hear a lot of things it been trying to tell you.

YOUR BODY IS NOT JUST A TOOL

When the world places so much emphasis on what our bodies look like, the first reaction is often to jump the old adage, "It's what inside that counts." In this way, the body is pitched as just shell for a human hermit crab. I myself used to think this. Google my name and you'll find tons of eloquent quotes about how my body was house or a storage unit, and it is what was stored on inside that really mattered. Man, was I wrong.

Reducing our bodies to just a storage unit or shell of what we are as an individual cheapens our existence. Right now, close your eyes. Feel the temperature in the room. Maybe you hear something in the background, like a bird or a car passing. Maybe your shirt is soft against your skin. Maybe it causes you to itch. How does this make you feel?

Many of the ways we experience life and even how we express our emotions come through our bodies. Take, for example, when you are sad or upset. Your mind is feeling the emotional stress and might start to produce tears. These tears help you communicate non-verbally your current emotional state. Your nose might begin to run—that's your body draining the tears out of your eye so you can still see.[60] Then your body may start producing hormones that calm you and purge the toxins that manage stress.[61] Your body is helping you process your emotion. It's the perfect example of why we can't just separate the mind and the body.

I like to think of people as computer games—this is obviously the product of my nerd upbringing. To make a computer game, you need back-end code and front end code. Back-end code tells the game what actions to take as a result of your inputs. "If the player presses A, then the character jumps." It's the brain of a program. Front end code is the body. "If the character is jumping, move this piece of the game in this way." It explains how you see the program and how your gameplay translates into visuals. Every front end code is unique and specific to the back-end code, and you need both for either to be useful. You can't play a video game you can't see, and you can't move a character if you have no way to tell it to move. That's an oversimplified explanation, but it will do for this analogy.

Just like a video game, we can't live life if we cannot physically experience it; and we cannot make meaningful use of our bodies without direction from our minds. We often neglect to realize all the ways our body supports us, and instead get caught up in the way it prevents us from doing what we want or think we deserve to have. Furthermore, this means that our thoughts, feelings, and attitudes affect our biological functioning and how we use our physical body affects our mental state. The body and mind have a complex interdependence, and valuing one over the other cheats us out of our ability to live our best lives.[62]

EVERYONE IS DIFFERENT

Way back in the beginning of this book, we talked about how each of our personalities and identities were different, based on how we were raised, genetics, our life experiences, and so much more. Well, the exact same thing is true for our bodies. As much as you might think there is a perfect body that you can have if you just work hard enough, that is not the case. The "perfect body" marketed to you by magazines, advertisements, and social media is a lie. And just like each body is different, so are the ways in which that body will be able to experience and enjoy movement.

How you move is determined by a variety of different things, like your body composition, the shape of your bones, and even your mental state. If you're tall, you may find it harder to lift the same amount as shorter person, simply because you have lug that weight a longer distance. Rocking a rounder-than-average rump? You might find it hard to run as fast as others. Top-heavy? You might have a more hunched posture. Struggling with depression? You might find you feel physically exhausted and tired. Running from zombies to save your life? Your adrenaline may cause you to be faster, stronger, and more coordinated than usual.

The point is that there will always be different types of movements that are harder to do and types that are easier, based on your unique self. It is impossible for every person to be good at everything—we all have limitations. We also have things that we are more likely to be good at. It all depends on the situation we are in. The thing to focus on is that there is always something you can excel at, no matter what your body is like.

I love doing yoga and have practiced it somewhat religiously over the past five years. However, as much as I love it, there are some poses that my body is physically incapable of doing. As a plus-size woman with self-described candy juicy thighs, paired with the calf muscles of a sexy lady hulk, I am unable to touch my heel to the back of my leg. I have flesh and muscle that forms a stronger barrier than the security guards at [insert cool and trendy pop artist's] concert. I could get angry about it, or I could instead focus on doing what I can do. Like—I've got amazing back and hip flexibility. I can't bow pose for the life of me, but I can distract anyone who's concerned with that by popping into the splits.

Why am I telling you all of this? Because there is going to be types of movement you hate. There are going to be activities you suck at, fail at, and curse their existence. That doesn't mean all movement is bad. It just means you haven't found the right movement for you. Instead of trying to pick up the latest exercise trend du jour, ask yourself, "How can I move in a way that benefits and pleases me— whatever that might mean for my unique self."

When you first start exploring exercise, it's important to recognize that you will not be good at or enjoy some activities. I have met so many women who don't exercise because they went to the gym and felt uncomfortable, or tried to run and couldn't keep up with the run club they had joined. I am sure that as I type this, you are thinking of a similar experience where you too have felt overwhelmed by trying a new type of movement. It has happened to us all.

If you are just getting started exploring moving more, you might want to test your body's current abilities at home. Try a variety of simple stretches and movements to assess your flexibility, stamina, and coordination. Take time to feel the movements, and note which your body most positively reacts to. At-home explorations can be an amazing first step toward a more active lifestyle, as it removes the pressures public exercising can bring. Additionally, you can move at your own pace and really listen intently to how your body feels and your mind reacts to different movements.

As you work through different activities, ask yourself one very important question—"Do I enjoy this form of movement?" You may have it in your mind that movement has to be a cumbersome, loathsome activity and that if it doesn't feel like some sort of medieval torture it's not beneficial. However, that's simply not the case. Movement is movement. When expanding beyond your at-home effort, try exploring a wide array of new activities and avoiding those activities you've struggled with in the past. If you try something new and it doesn't work for you, don't swear off exercise completely; just move on. Keep trying new activities until you find movement that is enjoyable and meaningful. You might even surprise yourself and discover things you didn't even know you are good at or didn't think you'd enjoy!

How to Get Started Moving More

1. Explore: Explore movement at home to uncover skills and challenges to how you move.

2. Experience: Try a variety of movements until you find one you enjoy.

3. Commit: Make a small commitment to regularly do the movement you love.

4. Acknowledge: Recognize and celebrate the joy and sense of self this movement brings to your life.

5. Expand: Try new activities to your life using the previous four steps.

MAKING PEACE WITH YOUR BODY

You may feel like you're at war with your body. You tell it to do one thing, it rebels and does another. You try to make positive changes in your life, and it seems like its standing in the way. It can feel like you versus your body, and that's part of the problem. In order to fully embrace life and all it's wonderful opportunities, you need to find peace with your body. You need to stop wasting precious energy fighting yourself and instead find yourself.

Making peace with your body begins with acknowledging all the ways your body supports you daily, instead of all the ways you perceive it to hold you back. When you are faced with a negative body thought, pause and counter it with a functional positive about your body. It might be tempting to use phrases that speak to aesthetics such as "My body is beautiful" or "My face is attractive." These phrases are subjective and frankly will not help you remember the value and support your body provides you. Instead try to recognize how your body moves, is built or reacts in ways that help you in your day-to-day life.

For example, I have a large booty and thighs, and a common negative thought for me is that my legs are ugly because they are so disproportionately large. Mentally, I conquer this thought by reminding myself that a large bottom half helps me have better balance and supports me in activities I love that require it. The key isn't to try and turn a perceived negative about your body into a positive. It's about recognizing your body has value and worthy of your respect.

In line with this vein of thinking, daily affirmations of love, unprompted, can also help you build body confidence. Sit in front of the mirror and acknowledge at least one thing you like about your body—you can be as vain as you want. Have a body love-fest. Talk about your stunning eyes, your vicious curves, and your perfect hair. Be silly. Be positive. Enjoy celebrating your body.

Once you've successfully celebrated the sheer awesome that your body is, take time to thank it as well. Think of at least three ways your body has supported you that day. Think of activities you did, emotions you felt, or even how your body reacted to the weather. If you are struggling to come up with things in the beginning, you can always thank your body for breathing. It sounds simple, but your body every day takes the breaths you need to live. That's something pretty special you can always be grateful for.

This exercise will help you recognize how amazing your body is on a daily basis. Over time, you'll find that you naturally begin to notice how your body supports you in your day-to-day life, even when you're away from the mirror.

Another way to recognize your body's power is to mindfully meditate and recognize all the wonderful things your body helps you feel, learn, and experience. I recommend body scan meditation if you want to explore a guided practice. It will prompt you to focus your mind on various ways your body is interacting with the world. Body-focused meditation is great to do before bed, as it also helps you to release pent-up tension in our body. The result is a more restful sleep and a better start to your day.[63]

Lastly, and this might sound vain, but dress in clothing you love. Ditch the clothing rules. Don't buy a smaller size of dress to earn through weight loss. Do not punish yourself for not looking the way you think you need to be worthy of nice things. Waiting to wear something you love is a daily reminder that your body is not yet worthy of celebration. It's a reminder that your body is still the enemy. This practice of earning the right to wear things is preached to us as a reward, but is actually an undeserved punishment when we need encouragement most.

The better you become at recognizing your body's benefits, the more protective you will become of it. You will also begin to realize that a stranger will never know your body and how it reacts as well as you do. You'll be less likely to succumb to marketing and scare tactics that prey on your body insecurities. You'll also be better able to make the right choices that benefit your body, and less susceptible to body trends and diet culture. When you know your body, you can make the best and most fulfilling choices for it.

Ways to Make Peace with Your Body

1. Reframe negative self-talk.

2. Practice daily body praise and gratitude.

3. Connect with your body through meditation.

4. Dress how you love; ditch the "when I deserve it" mentality.

CHAPTER 10

CHALLENGES: STRESS AND OTHER NO-GOOD, ROTTEN THINGS

"The pessimist sees difficulty in every opportunity, the optimist sees opportunity in every difficulty."

—Winston Churchill

In middle school, I played intramural basketball and sang a full-bodied alto in the school choir. One-not so-fateful evening, I just so happened to have a choral extravaganza scheduled for just an hour after a basketball game. I had sixty minutes to strip down, shower, redress, primp and high-tail it back to the school. This might have been a challenge for an everyday child in secondary school, but not for one Anna O'Brien. I had speed. I had determination. I had yet to develop an evolved self-care and beauty routine.

As soon as I entered the house after the game, I sprang into action. In record speed, I flung my basketball uniform onto the floor, turned the shower on to a suitable warmth, and before you could sing the lyrics to an entire Fleetwood Mac song, I was blow drying my hair. I was crushing it. As I pulled my curling iron out to give my hair just a little "I'm singing a solo in a semi-important school event" sparkle, my mom yelled at me from down below.

"Anna, you have *five* minutes and whatever you do don't leave the curling iron on. *Do. Not. Leave. The Curling. Iron. On.*" I made my promise and continued to speed transform my hair into fancy-as-can-be ringlets of choral perfection. Within just a few minutes, I was done; I tossed on clean, performance-ready attire and was on my way to dazzle the parents of Kenston Middle School with my vocal rendition of a poorly arranged selection of upbeat disco songs.

The performance went as well as a middle-school performance could go and we found our way headed back to our cul de sac house in suburban Ohio. As we rounded the corner onto the street where we lived, we saw them— two bright red shiny fire trucks parked in our circular driveway. My mother immediately smacked me. "I told you not to leave the curling iron on." But it wasn't the curling iron that started the blaze, it was something much worse.

As we entered the house a fire man stood talking to my father. "We believe this to be the cause of the fire," he said, holding up a charred bit of elastic. I knew that elastic. It was my underwear. I had accidently thrown my bikini briefs on a lamp, and the direct contact with the light had set them ablaze.

Challenges find you in the most unusual and unexpected ways. Just as I couldn't anticipate my underwear literally setting my house on fire—there will be challenges in your life that, even though you are doing everything you possibly can right, show up and wreak havoc. The underwear incident was just my first unusual experience of many. I've been trapped in a snow avalanche, lost in a foreign country, had my apartment flood, and split my pants on the Vegas Strip. I've also experienced trauma like losing my mother and sister, being robbed while home, and accidently ending up in the middle of a knife fight. The amount of crazy and at times downright depressing things life has thrown at me has even earned me the endearing nickname Calamity Jane. Wherever I am, there's a calamity on the horizon.

I suppose we all feel that way at times. Life is full of challenges. In this chapter we'll discuss how challenges shape us, learn strategies for surviving the worst, and discuss how to turn setbacks into opportunities.

WHAT CHALLENGES ARE GOOD FOR

Probably the most annoying thing I will write in this book lives in this chapter under this sub-header. Ready for it? Challenges make you great. Yes, I am sure you have heard it before. I'm sure you've heard it every time you didn't win a game or didn't get a part in the school play. I'm sure you've heard it at work and school, and probably even at home. On Sundays, if you're religious, you've heard it at church.

The problem with the phrase is that no one ever seems to explain why challenges are good for us. I hope to rectify that very problem right here and now, so at the very least I can get you to stop rolling your eyes and to start paying attention again. If you have a gem and you want to make it sparkle, you must first literally buff it with friction and pressure until it's smooth. If you want a knife to be sharp, you have to strike it against a stone over and until a new edge is carved. If you want to grow a beautiful, strong flower you have to bury a seed in a literal mix of feces, garbage, and dead plants for it to grow. Struggle is simply part of greatness.

Let's dive deeper than just a few metaphors, and explore why embracing and facing our challenges make us our best selves. We can't always choose what we will be burdened with, but we can choose how we react to it. Struggles challenge our minds, force us to take leaps of faith, build our relationships with others, help us develop new skills, and work—and give us ongoing feedback on our efforts. Without struggles, there is no growth. In fact, all learning comes from struggle. The smartest people you know are likely those who have struggled the most. It is our challenges that make us great.

Struggles force you to focus and drive your brain into action. Psychologists often recommend individuals take on new activities if they are feeling stagnant in life. A new hobby is just a mini-challenge in disguise. It's a new skill to learn. Challenges, simply put, keep your brain happy and prevent you from feeling bored or stuck.

Nobody is perfect at everything (even though some people think they are). Sometimes you are faced with challenges that you find you simply don't have the skills to overcome on your own. In that way, these issues create logical and easy ways for you to bond with your community and strengthen relationships. When you interact with your community while overcoming challenges, you begin to give and share feedback allowing you all to further optimize and improve your lives more consistently. You begin to recognize and become grateful for the presence of others in your lives as well. As a result, both you and those you interact with benefit from new learning and a broader understanding of community. Struggle in this way builds empathy, compassion, and gratitude.

Four Reasons Struggle Is Good for You

1. We learn through struggle.

2. It keeps us from getting bored.

3. It helps us build relationships.

4. It serves as a foundation for empathy.

ENDURE IT OR FIX IT

There are two types of challenges: those we must endure and those we must change. Though I am not a specifically religious person, I have always appreciated the beginning of the Serenity Prayer. "Grant me the serenity to accept the things I cannot change; courage to change the things I can; and wisdom to know the difference." It's like the entire human struggle, wrapped up in a single sentence. It's simple, but as we both know, is oh so hard to actually live by.

The things we cannot change are things like death, physical and mental challenges, and natural disasters. These challenges often happen due to no fault of our own. Many people are born with mental health issues, and while they can treat them, they can't be just magically taken away. The challenge isn't to erase them, but rather to learn to accept and endure them as best we can. Similarly, when someone has passed you can't bring them to life and you certainly can't replace them with someone new. For these types of challenges, we must learn how to endure and make the best of the test and trials that come into our lives as a result.

Also included in this category are people. A hard lesson many of us have learned is that you cannot change someone else. You might be well intention and determined. You might really love them. They might really love you, No matter what the only person that can change someone is themselves. In this way other people can present challenges into your life that you cannot control but must endure or separate yourself from. And often time in these situations we are trading the challenge of a toxic relationship for the pain of a loss of friendship. When it comes to the things we cannot change, there often aren't a lot of easy answers.

However there is good news! The second category of challenges are things that we can change, have decision in the final outcome and or can remove from our life entirely. These make up the majority of challenges we face. Disagreements with friends/coworkers, failure, underdeveloped skills and abilities often fall in this category. These are the challenges that inspire you to reach for stars, dream big, never give up and whatever other two-to-four-word phrase you've seen on an inspirational poster in a public high school counselors office.

CHALLENGES AND OPPORTUNITIES

When I was younger the idea of crafting was so exciting. I remember buying puffy paints, and pom-poms and all sorts of sparkles. I was ready to design the best handicraft T-shirt on the block. People we're going to come from miles around to see this shirt. So I took my fresh white tee and I got to work. Unfortunately, things didn't go as planned. One hour in and my white T-shirt looked like it had unsuccessfully served as the white flag in a craft store war. I spent three more hours trying to fix the shirt and make it the masterpiece I had imagined in my head. The shirt began to become a chunky mess of all my failed attempts at glory.

I was devastated...for like thirty minutes. That was about how long it took me to realize I needed to get out of the crafting world and into the supply world. I gathered up all the junk I had left to from my fashion war, repackaged them, and took them to school to sell. It began with craft supplies and soon extended to things out of an Oriental Trading Company catalog. Eventually I progressed to beanie babies, getting in ahead of the trend and making enough sales at consignment stores as a fourteen-year-old to finance a year abroad.

Regardless of whether we can fix a challenge or not, each struggle we face can present us with unexpected opportunities for growth, whether it be with personal development, professionally, etc. The first step is to look at yourself as a problem-solver. Yes, you, are your own life's Navy SEAL, SWAT team leader, Green Beret, and whatever other reference for cool person who solves problems under pressure I forgot. If you want all those shiny metallic linings of those crummy-day clouds, you're going to have to go looking for them. Start by reframing your current challenges as opportunities you need to solve for, like an algebra problem. Focusing on the negatives of the current situation can hurt our self-confidence and deter us from overcoming challenges. So instead of saying, "I lost my job and I can't pay my bills," instead say something like, "I want to find a new career I love that allows me to live comfortably." The second sentence gives you a clearly defined identity goal to work toward.

The key is to remind yourself every day, "I am a problem-solver." It's super-hard, but try to approach every day as an opportunity to make things a little bit better in your life. Instead of running from problems in your life, acknowledge them head-on. Sometimes wallowing in the problem can feel so good, but it doesn't actually help us. The average person actually complains once per minute[64] when in conversation—once a minute! That's a whole lot of complaining! However research shows that complaining actually makes people feel worse—both you and the people you complain to.[65] It also slows down your brain's ability to actually solve the problem at hand by shrinking your hippocampus,[66] the part of your brain essential for intelligent thought. Staying stuck in a problem is like trading long-term stability and happiness for short-term sympathy. If you have to complain, do it strategically—to get the support you need to resolve the issue at hand.

You cannot predict how a problem will be solved. This is a hard lesson to learn. We have all done it. You have a challenge in your life and you immediately begin to try and emulate how Suzy down the street conquered it or how your favorite YouTuber made it work. Problems and the context surrounding them are not generic, and neither are their solutions. Instead of focusing on the approach or even the problem itself, focus on the outcome—what do I want to achieve? First, this resets your brain from thinking about the past (the problem) and focuses it on your future (the ideal outcome). You're much better suited to make decisions about your future when you are actually focused on it. You'll find that you discover a whole new list of ways you could try to achieve your goal, without having someone else's history or the problem dragging down your focus on success.

Finding opportunities in challenges means paying attention to your skills, trying new things, and not feeling overwhelmed by failure. Some things you will want to fight for—regardless of whether you have the skills or not. Those are the rare Michael Jordan basketball story moments— where passion and perseverance lead to success. However, in most cases we simply keep repeating the same thing over and over because we haven't given ourselves a little space to think about the problem differently. If you can, separate yourself from the problem and allow your mind to get creative; you might surprise yourself with a whole new idea. Opportunities in life are often missed, not because you weren't in the right place at the right time, but because you were too focused on something else to see them.

How to Turn Challenges Into Opportunities

1. Think like a problem-solver.

2. Complain only when strategic.

3. Focus on the future, versus the past.

4. If something's not working, change up your approach.

WHY YOU STRESSIN'?

When I was in my final year of college, I was, in short, a hot mess. I was nervous about not having the internship I needed to actually graduate. I was very aware that I had no job, no money, and no place to live as soon as I took that apparently super-fulfilling walk across the podium and grabbed my degree. I was also deeply immersed in a competitive senior project that my Type A personality had committed to win, even though the only prize of winning seemed to be lack of sleep. I was basically Oscar the Grouch, living in a garbage can filled with emotions, anxiety and stress.

It was after a particularly bad day that my best friend and roommate, Tracie, tried to discuss the cleanliness of our apartment. The current state was a war zone of random food wrappers and neon green fur scraps left from the alien characters I was sewing for my advertising final. We have all been there. That lovely point where life becomes so challenging and overwhelming that your day-to-day becomes an act of survival. "I know you're stressed, but you need to clean this up," Tracie said in a bizarre tone, a mix of kindness and annoyance. It was then that the ticking time bomb of stress exploded inside me. I screamed. I whined. I stomped off to my room like a petulant child. It was a miracle I didn't slam the door.

As I sat in my room I started to stew over how cruel Tracie had been. If she wanted a clean apartment—she could clean it! However, as you probably well know, when you sit long enough with your thoughts, you begin to think about things you've been avoiding. You also realize the people you've taken them out on, like a good friend, who just wanted a clean living space. Just as the guilt was setting in, I heard a ghostly, giggly voice pipe through my air vent, "*ANNNNNNNA*, you want to take Tracie to Sonic because you are *sorrrrrry* and she's sorry too." Our relationship was as resilient as we were weird.

Often when you are experiencing lots of challenges coupled together you also experience lots of stress and lash out at the people you love most; the people you expect will forgive you regardless of how much of a no-good jerk face you act like. While these outbursts give you a temporary sense of relief, they do not help you find move through or fix or problems. Managing the stress you experience as a result of a challenge or trauma requires you to recognize what is causing you to feel overwhelmed directly, acknowledge how that feeling might be changing how you act, and react to things and how that behaviors may be affecting your well-being.

Now, stress associated with challenges can affect us uniquely in lot of different ways, but psychologists like to categorize them into three groups: acute, episodic and chronic. Understanding these three categories can help you deal with stress better and know when to seek outside help in coping.

The first form of stress, acute, is the most common type of stress you experience. Acute stress is usually a result of your daily demands and general life pressure and only occurs for short periods of time. It's the stress you feel when you're late for work, can't find your car keys, or when you forgot to eat breakfast, it's 3 p.m. and you're hangry. Symptoms from acute stress aren't usually that present, unless stress has accumulated. When you feel short waves of annoyance, anxiousness, or irritability, that's likely a result your pent-up acute stress expressing itself.

Unlike the other types of stress we'll discuss, acute stress isn't always negative. It is also the clanging the heart you feel before you go down a big hill on a roller-coaster, the nervous anticipation of a bachelorette weekend, and the restless excitement when you know someone will love the birthday present you picked out for them. In these examples, the acute stress acts as catalyst and proxy of excitement. It also can cause your body to release adrenaline, which helps us focus and enhances our overall experience.

The next type of stress you may experience is episodic stress. Have you ever found yourself buried in responsibilities, without anyway to dig yourself out? Somehow you managed to sign up for the bake sale, organizing a work potluck, joined an adult soccer league, volunteered to knit blankets for orphan children, agreed to mentor fifteen interns, committed to writing a book, held down a full time job, and rescued three new puppies at the same time. Ok, so maybe that was a bit of an exaggeration.

However, If you're a Type A perfectionist, you're probably all too familiar with this type of stress as it manifests as a result of self-induced, unrealistic, and/or illogical expectations. It's the result of too much to do and too little time to do it in.

Episodic stress can cause you to feel overwhelmed and lead to ceaseless worrying. With so many things on your plate, you'll constantly be stressing out about possibility of one them going awry. This can lead to episodes of depression, headaches, and anxiety. It also can do a number on our hearts, such as causing coronary heart disease among other things.

When dealing with episodic stress, you have to let yourself slow down. This may sound impossible to your little Type A soul, but you need to say "No" to new projects and "Yes" to self-care and buffer time. With less on your plate, you'll have space to remove a lot of the worry around the projects you do keep with a little room to spare for unexpected things that pop into your life outside of your control. In some cases, you may need professional help to learn to manage the cycles of depression and anxiety associated with this form of stress.

The last form, chronic stress, is the most severe and is the polar opposite of acute stress. It's never exciting. It's destructive and dangerous, and it can control your life if not dealt with. Chronic stress is so severe it can significantly alter you mind, body, and soul.

It should make sense given the severity of chronic stress is merely equal to the experiences that cause it. This form of distress is a result of major life challenges such as toxic and abusive relationships, chronic illness, war, and poverty. The symptoms of chronic illness feel never-ending and impossible to overcome. Common symptoms include difficulty breathing, increased heart rate, insomnia, fatigue, and more. In some cases, the stress becomes so overwhelming that the individual experiencing the pressure feels they can only overcome it by destroying themselves or their body. It is chronic stress that leads to major depression, PTSD, serious heart illness, and even, in some cases, cancer.[67]

You can try to reduce chronic stress by engaging in basic health behaviors, such as sleeping more regularly, participating in daily physical activity, and reducing stimulants such as caffeine, nicotine, and/or sugar. The reality is, however, that chronic stress most often requires professional help to manage and deal with. If you constantly feel overwhelmed, struggle to get through your daily routine, feel depressed about your future, or hopeless in general you should seek consultation with a licensed mental health professional. Mental health professionals can help you develop behaviors and patterns to reduce the effect chronic stress has on your happiness.

How to Deal with Different Types of Stress

1. Acute: Experience it and acknowledge it is only temporary.

2. Episodic: Reduce commitments and increase self-care.

3. Chronic: Episodic treatments, reduce stimulants, and see a professional.

CHAPTER 11

RELATIONSHIPS: FRIENDS, FAMILY, AND LOVERS

"Things are never quite as scary when you've got a best friend."

—Bill Watterson

Growing up I had a best friend named Ashley. Our parents were friends from church, and as a result our families spent a lot of time together. Even though she was a year younger than me, she was one of my closest friends and unofficial partner in crime as a child. Even more importantly, Ashley saw my life in its rawest form. When things were rough at home, when I was out of control and so far from normal, she stayed a friend. I can think back to specific times in my past where I legitimately felt Ashley was the only one who cared if I lived or died. In a lot of ways, her friendship saved me.

It had been hard going to college without her, so naturally I was elated to find that upon graduation she'd be going to the same university. I imagined it would be just like elementary through high school—going to amusement parks, games of tacky Barbie runway show, and waiting in line to be first to see Ben Folds. I'd have my best friend back. I had started to blossom in college, and I was excited for her to see how much I'd changed.

At first, we saw each often, but not too much. She was a freshman living in the dorms, and I was living up the road at Portuguese language immersion housing. She would visit often. Even though we didn't hang out as often as we once had, I felt we were still kindred spirits. Slowly but surely, things began to change. She started to hang out with a few indie filmmaker cool kids in her class. I saw her less. Still, when we were together we seemed to have the same silly fun we'd always had. I convinced myself that I was just overthinking it all. Nothing feels worse than the fear of losing someone you love, and I am sure you, like I, can remember a time just like this. The moment things started to change.

One night in the summer, we went to see a play together. It felt like it always had, two friends laughing together and cracking jokes. As we went home, Ashley offered me a ride on her scooter. As we took a hairpin U-turn, too tight for a scooter with a large-rumped lady on the back to clear, her bike fell over. I apologized profusely and offered to pay for any service it might need. She brushed it off and proceeded to drop me off at home. This would be the last time Ashley ever spoke to me.

I called. I tweeted. I Facebooked. I emailed. In return she blocked, ignored, and deleted me out of her life. Fifteen years of friendship gone in a poof. I couldn't explain it and she didn't feel I needed or deserved an explanation. When Ashley walked out of my life, she didn't only take away her presence—she took away my ability to trust others with the vulnerable parts of my life. Ashley had put up a wall between us, and I had put a wall up between my heart and the world.

In time, I was able to heal and rebuild my ability to trust through other great friendships, but still to this day I am hesitant as to who I allow in the inner circle. I learned in a very jarring way that relationships change you. They can make you stronger. They can break you. They can challenge you. And just as much they can alter your worldview, how you treat your own relationships can and will affect others.

In this chapter, we'll explore relationships—your lovers, family, and friends. We'll talk about the types of relationships, why they are important, and how they affect your life. We'll also discuss how to tend your own relationship garden—how to build new relationships, recognize when a relationship needs nurturing, and walk away when a relationship has become toxic.

THE BULLSEYE OF INTERPERSONAL RELATIONSHIPS

Have you ever been at a party chatting with your friends about the latest internet meme or how Ms. Famous-pants just accidentally mooned the Queen and someone juts into the conversation and it just feels uncomfortable? It's not that the person entering the conversation is bad or unusual in any way, it's simply because they've crossed a boundary line in what I like to call the relationship bullseye.

Coworker. Family member. Lover. Best friend. Book Club partner. Teacher. The types of relationships we have are almost endless. Furthermore, many of these relationships aren't mutually exclusive. You can have a family member that is also your teacher. You can have a book club partner who is also your best friend. You can have a coworker who's also your lover—oh, the scandal! Instead of trying to make sense of 47,823 variations, with 39,156 ways they can manifest,[68] and three hundred different things each one can be called, it's easier to look at our relationships in terms of their depth.

Think of all your relationships as a bullseye. At the core you have your Champions—those who know you and your secrets and desires, and support you through thick and thin. The next ring out you have your confidants, those you trust with personal information, history, and your more complex emotions. The third ring is your Community, who you trust with information about your life, activities, and everyday experiences. The fourth group is your Connections, a group people who you are connected to regarding a topic or interest, but share very little information or emotion with outside of what is relevant to that specific discussion. The last and most broadly applicable circle are your Contacts. These are the everyday people we encounter and with whom we have enjoyable, but shallow, purpose-based interactions.

THE RELATIONSHIP BULLSEYE

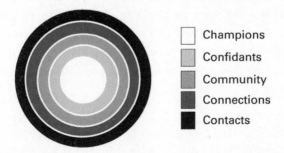

☐ Champions
☐ Confidants
☐ Community
☐ Connections
■ Contacts

Champions are your most intimate relationships, your ride-or-die tribe, and your trustworthy secret keepers. They've known you at your worst, cheered you on at your best, and held your hand through trauma. They know your past and are invested in your future. When a person describes another as "their rock," they're talking about their Champions. For example, you might feel comfortable telling your partner or best friend about your work challenges, you monthly visit from Aunt Flo, and your feelings on the drama within your friend group. Champions help us process and recognize challenges and opportunities in our other relationships.

Research conducted by the University of Virginia studied how people's brains reacted when they were under threat of receiving small electrical shocks to either themselves, a close friend, or a stranger. The findings were astonishing. The brain activity of when you are in the person in danger versus when you know your friend is essentially the same. "Our self comes to include who we become close to," explained James Coan, the director of the study. Champions aren't just close friends, they are extension of who we are.[69]

TV would have you believe that you should have a close knit, diverse friend group of no less than five people that make up your personal pool of Champions. The truth is that these types of people will be rare in your life. According to research from Cornell University the average adult will only have two people in their life they would consider Champions.[70]

Confidants are like Champions, but less information is shared. Confidants might know a private information about a specific part of your life, versus getting the full spectrum view a Champion is likely to see. You might speak to one group of Confidants about your professional life and a completely separate group about your health challenges. Confidants are usually members of your community that have proven themselves trustworthy over time and as a result have shifted from a casual interaction to a more deeply personal one.

Community members are individuals you interact with on a day-to-day basis and share surface-level information about your life with, like your plans for the week or your thoughts on the latest season of *The Bachelor*. For example, you might tell your teammate at work about your plans for Friday night or have a discussion with your friend in barre class about how much you want another dog. These conversations provide some personal details, but are shallow. Your secrets are protected. That's because we don't fully trust members of our community. This is not necessarily because they are bad people, but because we don't have enough experience or history to determine if they are a safe space to share deeper parts of our lives and emotions.

Unlike the Community relationship, where conversation is broad and shallow, Connections are people we engage with solely around a shared interest. For example, let's say you have a dog that you take to the dog park. At the dog park, you're likely to see some of the same owners (and their dogs) on a regular basis. After a while, you'd likely know a ton about their dogs and when they usually come to the park, but it's unlikely that you'd know much more about their life. You also are unlikely to see any of them outside of an activity involving your dogs. In this case your dog is the topic that has allowed these Connections to form.

The last ring of the relationship bullseye is our Contacts. These are the shallowest of our relationships, and are marked simply by coming into contact with a person on a regular basis. In this way, the relationship exists out of the contact exchange. As a result, the discussion and information shared is rarely more than a "Hello" or an exchange of information required for you to complete a transaction. Your favorite barista at a Starbucks is a great example of a Contact.

The reason the bullseye of relationships is helpful is because it helps us understand the common boundaries and depth that relationships have. Oftentimes, when a relationship goes awry it's because a friend's expectations and your assessment of where the friendship is doesn't align. A study by Tel Aviv University found that only 50 percent of friendships are actually reciprocated, compared to the 95 percent who thought their friendships were mutually strong.[71] What this means is that most people are both terrible at communicating their own relationship boundaries and at perceiving others'. Helping communicate, recognize, and establish clear boundaries in your relationships will strengthen and make your most valued relationships more meaningful.

GETTING NEEDY ABOUT OUR INTIMACY

I once dated a guy where things initially were awesome. We got on well, were attracted to each other, and generally liked the same things. However as time went on, I found myself disinterested in him. I could not figure out why. On the magical checklist of things that we are told our partners should be, he checked all the boxes. He was tall, handsome, and strong. He was employed, smart, and kind. He respected my rights. Like, literally most straight women would die to meet a chap like him, and there I was, trying to figure out why I wanted to walk away.

We are told that ideal relationships are charted in checklists of characteristics that make up our perfect friend or mate. Magazines thrive on quizzes that ask mundane things like your favorite ice cream flavor, when you last danced at a party, and how many scrunchies you own, trying to predict what you need in a partner. Television convinces us that in order to build a close relationship with a new friend we need to be just like them. Relationships are shown as shallow. However, lasting, long-term relationships, whether they are with friends, lovers, or even family, exist because we meet each other's needs. Now, while relationships can have a bevy of unique needs, there are three universal needs we all strive for: companionship (I belong), affection (I am desired) and emotion (I matter). These make up the backbone of lasting relationships.

Ever meet a friend one day and instantly know you are meant to be best friends for life? You finish each other's sentences, and you both know and love that super-obscure Australian comedy show about high school. When you are with this person, you feel comfortable and open with who you are. You also feel like your friend/partner/family is focused and aware of your needs. If your companionship needs are being met by a relationship, you feel like you belong. As we discussed in previous chapters, belonging is one of your fundamental needs as a human. Maslow, famous for describing the human hierarchy of needs, found that companionship was such a strong need that in certain situations—especially traumatic ones—that it can outweigh our basic needs and safety.[72]

Affection is often viewed in contrast to companionship, mostly by glossy magazines which exhaust the age-old discussion of which is better—sex or intimacy? The hard truth is both. While companionship makes us feel like we belong, affection is all about desire (*bow-chicka bow-wow*). Now I might have led you a little astray here, because affection doesn't actually have to be sexual at all. Affection is communicated from looks, actions, words, and touch. It can be the way your rescue pup stares at you when you return home from a long day away or the how a partner holds you in their arms. Affection is most often associated with how we display love.

Lastly, close relationships require there to be emotional support between the two parties. This is where things get real. A relationship that provides emotional support makes both parties feel like their opinions, feelings, and experiences matter and is the ethos of the connection. Often, you begin new friendships by showing how much you care about their general well-being. This establishes an emotional tenderness to your connection which establishes the fact that you support each other. Emotional support is particularly interesting because it is not triggered as a result of any specific action. You can feel emotionally supported just by reflecting on an individual, even though you may not have had a recent interaction. Just like we have a personal emotional bank account, each relationship will have also has a similar structure. The more you make deposits, by showing we genuinely care about them and their experiences, the more the individual can draw upon those actions, words, and thoughts to determine they are emotionally supported.

If I think back to the previously mentioned relationship with my dreamboat of a supposedly perfect man, but now with this new lens, it's clear why it didn't work. While he was a great companion and super affectionate, I didn't feel like my emotional needs were being met. He wasn't able to be fully open and share that side of himself with me, and a result the relationship felt off-kilter and unfulfilling. When you begin to see your relationships falter or you no longer feel they are rewarding, it's usually because one or more of these needs are not being met for you or your friend/partner. When that balance is shifted completely to one individual and the fulfillment of their needs begins to have priority over the other's, that is when a relationship can become toxic.

Three Universal Relationship Needs

1. Companionship: "I belong."

2. Affection: "I am desired."

3. Emotional Support: "I matter."

MAKING NEW FRIENDS AND KEEPING THE OLD

When I was a child, I often would meet another child, and within ten minutes we were holding hands and sharing graham crackers. Making friends as a wee little one is easy. However, it seems like with each year we age, making new friends gets harder and harder. Suddenly you're an adult, and forming a friendship somehow shifts to the equivalent of some giant hedge maze, with complex physical challenges, bizarre mental twists, and unpredictable outcomes. It can feel impossible.

The reason making friends is so much harder when you age is that you meet less people. You've become too busy, there's a bevy of ultra-important adult priorities that get in the way, and you're simply increasingly exhausted and don't have the energy. Pile on top the fact that you likely have years of experiences with previous relationships that have taught you the painful lesson that with each relationship there is a chance it could go south and lead to rejection, exploitation, or even destruction. New friendships are unpredictable and scary.

You're probably thinking to yourself, "Great you've just reminded me of exactly why a life of continued solitude is actually good thing. Now I can stay a hermit forever." As completely terrifying as it seems—and to be honest it actually is terrifying—having strong relationships as an adult is essential to your future happiness and well-being. You may already have friends, which is great. However, as we grow and change in life, so do our relationships. Some of those amazing friendships you have now may fade, and it's likely your life could always benefit from a few new faces. Adults with a strong set of relationships are more likely to be healthy (both mentally and physically) and live longer than those with fewer connections.[73] Also, a recent study found that healthy, diverse social interactions are like a happiness drug.

Making new friends can feel overwhelming, but it's not impossible to do. To meet new people you have to switch up your routine. The easiest place to start is saying "Yes" more frequently to the things existing friends and coworkers invite you to. If you're like me, most of the time after a long day you just want to go home, drink wine, and watch some bad reality TV while catching up on social media. The last thing you want to do is grab drinks, or go to an art show, or take a night run. However, every time you turn down group social interaction you are turning down opportunities to meet new people and make new friends. You might crack a joke at the art opening and find that your future new best friend laughs at it.

Another way to switch up your routine and expose yourself to new people is to explore something you love and enjoy. Try exploring an interest or take up a new hobby. Take up pottery. Try improv. Volunteer for a community service group. Join a library book club. Taking up a new hobby is an easy way to expose yourself to new surroundings and to new groups of people, in a way that is enjoyable. Plus, you're more likely to strike up a conversation when you get to talk about something you're already interested in.

Another way to meet new people is to change your daily patterns. This may be uncomfortable for some, but simply going to the coffee shop at a different time of day, eating lunch at a different place, or walking our dog at a new dog park increases our opportunities to meet new people. When I feel particularly stuck, sometimes I just take my pup Data for a walk around the neighborhood. Animals are to friendships what the guy on the street twirling a glittery arrow is to Subway: they draw your attention in. Plus it's an easy point of entry for a stranger, because animals are always kinder and more forgiving than humans.

If you feel completely stuck, there are websites and apps such as MeetUp, Bumble Friends, and more that help people make friends. There you can find new activities to try with a stranger who might just be your new BFF. Just like dating, if the first encounter is awkward or uncomfortable—you never have to see those people again.

You get the benefits of being exposed to new people, without the long-term commitment that comes with starting a new hobby or meeting them as part of your daily routine.

Lastly, sometimes new friends can be found among the old friends we've simply lost touch with, other than a few haphazard social media messages on birthdays and other life milestones. Take a stroll through your Facebook or Instagram friends, and you might find a new old friend who is just what you need to rev up your friendship game. Online interaction is often shallow and doesn't give us the depth we need to feel supported, desired, and important. Clicking a "Like" button isn't the same as giving a hug. Leaving a comment for all to see isn't the same as a phone call. In many ways, social interactions maintain relationships, but fail to grow them. So to turn these digital contact into true friends, you're going to have to meet them face-to-face.

In January 2011, an artist named Tanja Hollander was sitting sat alone in her apartment, chatting with a friend over Facebook. She looked at her "Friends" list of 626 people and wondered, "How many of these people are actually my friends?" It was that thought that led Hollander to begin the "Are you my friend?" project, in which she sought to connect with and photograph each and every one of her Facebook friends. Hollander's project led to her visiting people in forty-three states, five countries, and 150 towns. What she found from her experiences is that many of these online relationships flourished and depended significantly through in-person contact. She found herself having new and amazing experiences that she would not have been exposed, to had she not made an effort to connect with each of these people in real life.[74]

How to Make Friends as an Adult

1. Start saying "Yes" more.

2. Invest in an Interest or passion.

3. Change up your daily routine.

4. Try out friend matchmaking apps and meet-up groups.

5. Look for gold in your existing digital contacts.

SHOULD THEY STAY OR SHOULD THEY GO NOW?

Perhaps even harder than making new friends is getting rid of unproductive or destructive relationships. Some of these relationships you won't even know are affecting you negatively, until you do the research to really examine them. It doesn't matter if they're lovers or friends — break-ups are hard. The first step to making sure you have the right balance of friends and interactions is to really understand who you're interacting with, how often, and how that's making you feel. Yep, you're going to have to pay attention to those emotions. Start by going through your calendar, address book, phone, or however you manage your connections and making a list of all the people you consider a friend. Then next to each person, write the pros and cons of interacting with that individual and how often you see them. For example, "I like hanging out with Suzy because she makes me laugh. I dislike hanging out with Suzy because I find I can't talk about deeper issues."

Pretty soon, you'll see that some people have loads of things you enjoy about them and few negatives, but you never see them. It's time to re-prioritize your friendships. Sure some people are harder to see due to schedule clashes or distance, but most relationships you make time for you'll find can flourish. You'll also find that there are people you simply don't enjoy that much that you are seeing far too often. In this scenario, it's likely your friend views the depth of your relationship differently than you do (which, as we previously discussed, happens 50 percent of the time). It's time to put some boundaries up.

The simplest way to enforce boundaries is to just decrease the amount of time you spend with these people. This for the most part will happen naturally as you calibrate your friendships. You'll begin to say "Yes" to other experiences, or reach out to those you want to deepen your relationship with. You will simply have less time. In most cases, you aren't cutting them completely out of your life; you're simply trying to adjust how often you see them in order to make sense of the depth of relationship you have. In the beginning this may feel uncomfortable, mean, and rude— especially if the other person's wants are greater than yours. However, this behavior is actually kind. It's crueler to encourage someone to continue to invest in deepening a friendship, when you know you full well you do not want to invest the same emotion and energy. If you keep trying to keep the friendship alive in its current state, it's likely to implode or become toxic.

Toxic relationships are the hardest to understand, the most difficult for us to break, and the most misunderstood challenges in our adult life. From my perspective, it is one of two imbalances which are most likely to create these painful and destructive relationships: (1) your perceived depth of relationship with another does not match how the partner perceives it; or (2) there is an imbalance in the needs structure, such that one or both individuals feel their needs are not only not being met, but are being actively compromised. If hanging out with someone makes you feel undervalued, isolated, undesired, or worthless, it's time to consider cutting ties and moving on.

However, it's not always that simple. Oftentimes, our history, past emotions, and our own mental health prevent us from recognizing these toxic relationships clearly. This is particularly a challenge in romantic relationships, where cultural expectations of partners add an extra layer of complexity. It's best in the most challenging situations—those which you want to salvage but are at a loss on how to do so—that you reach out to a professional for help and guidance. Last but not least, if someone hits you or regularly uses their words to belittle you, seek help immediately. A relationship based on fear is always toxic, and no person, no matter how terrible they might be, ever deserves to endure abuse in a relationship.

CHAPTER 12

I'M SORRY, YOU CAN'T BE PERFECT

"If I waited for perfection...I would never write a word."

—Margaret Atwood

When I was a teenager after a long, hard day, I would rush up the stairs to my room. I'd close my blinds and turn my stereo up. I'd lay in bed as the familiar song began: "Cuz we lost it all, nothing lasts forever, I'm sorry I can't be perfect..." The song echoed in my body as I struggled in a world where I was trying to chase a type of perfection I would never have. I would never have the perfect body. I would never be perfect at interacting with others. I would never be perfect at school. I felt I was constantly apologizing for all the ways I was imperfect.

The band was Simple Plan, and I suppose I am starting off this chapter in the most appropriate way: admitting my deeply imperfect love of terrible early 2000s emo rock. However I can't help but think of this song as I pen (well, type) this final chapter. Why did that song even exist? Who was perpetuating the idea that anyone could or should be perfect? Why did we need a deeply apologetic song about normal human error?

The short but not-so-sweet answer, and I've said it before several times now, is that we're all being lied to. I'm half kidding when I write that, but also it's kind of true. We spend most of our lives trying to become the perfect specimen of what our parents, our friends, our work, etc. need. We view failure as this ultimate death. Never give up. Always keep pushing to reach for the stars. What if we're not meant for the stars, but instead should be reaching for flowers?

In writing this book, one thing I learned stood out more than anything else. I am not perfect. You are not perfect. Life isn't about getting all things right. In fact, you will very rarely get everything right. Sometimes you will get nothing right. Most of the time, our life is an exciting mixture of failure and success. Life is about becoming better, not becoming the best. The former is a destination, while the latter is a lifelong journey.

In this chapter, we'll talk about why we feel so pushed to be perfect, how it's affecting our lives, and how unrealistic expectations of others affect them.

THE CURSE OF PERFECTIONISM

Perfectionism is the need to be perfect, or at least to appear to be perfect to others. That last part is important because many perfectionists feel their life is just an emotionally and physically exhausting façade and behind the curtain they feel like imposters.

In 2007, the friends and family members of people who had recently committed suicide were interviewed. More than half of the interviews described the deceased individual as a perfectionist.[75] This is just one of many studies that links perfectionist tendencies with increased depression and self-destruction.

While suicide might be the extreme potential outcome of a perfectionism, other analysis shows that these individuals' heightened fear of failure and making mistakes can prevent them from achieving the success they desire in the first place.[76] This becomes a terrible cycle of unfulfilled dreams. You want perfection, but your desire for perfection keeps you from being perfect. It's kind of overwhelming, when you think about it. Even more interesting is the surprising fact that the most successful people in business and life are those who are less likely to be perfectionists.[77]

In the technology world, where I worked for some ten years before accidentally becoming quasi-internet-famous, we always used to say, "Fail fast, fail smart." It wasn't until I was researching perfectionism that I really understood what that meant. Simply put, trust yourself more and make decisions fearlessly—even if making the wrong choice seems terrifying. If you make a decision faster, you might succeed. If you make the wrong decisions you can fail, learn from it, and make a better decision in the future. While the perfectionist is still debating which choice to make, you could be on your way to bigger and brighter things.

As a self-identified Type A personality, perfectionism stresses me out. I have to fight against my tendencies to try to do everything perfectly, which is not easy. When I focus on letting things go, I can find myself mentally trying to be perfect at not being perfect. Oh, the hilarity of it all.

Perfectionists don't just want their lives to be idyllic, they want everything to be perfect. The napkin should be folded this way. The hotel should be spotless. The glasses shouldn't have scratches. Perfectionists see the world for all the ways it isn't ideal, versus all the potential their life and the world around them have. This can make them very hard to be around, because they are always complaining. Nothing is ever good enough. They see fault in everything.

Perfectionists also feel like they have to give 100 percent of their life 100 percent of the time to 100 percent of the things they can do. They overschedule their time, overcommit, and sacrifice sleep and their own health to follow through on these unrealistic standards. A perfectionist believes, "I'll sleep when I'm done. I'll take care of myself when I finish this job." But the job is never done, because the work is never perfect. Instead, they experience burnout coupled with some other nasty side effects such as exploitation, isolation, depression, and stagnation. The extra stress perfectionists put on their body can also cause depression, eating disorders, and anxiety. In serious cases, this obsession with order has even triggered the development of Obsessive-Compulsive Disorder.

Perfectionists often tend to get exploited in professional and academic settings because by nature they will step in and take control of a project and ensure that it's delivered immaculately. The need to be perfect drives us to also crave control and oversight of every part of our lives. Perfectionists avoid delegating tasks to others because of their all-or-nothing mentality. They believe there is a right way and a wrong way to do everything. Their way is right, everyone else's is wrong. Because we're all human and what's "right" is highly subjective, others aren't necessarily going to see their point of view when they are working in a group. So the perfectionist just does it all themselves, so there is no opposition. Freeloaders live much of their life looking for their next perfectionist to offload work onto.

WHY PERFECT PEOPLE FAIL

Have you ever pulled an all-nighter to fix the alignment of a PowerPoint? Have you taken on project after project, because you feared that in someone else's hands they might slip through the cracks? Have you ever struggled to make a decision because making the right decision seemed more important than making a decision at all? If so, then welcome to the club. As the unofficial "Perfectionists and People Who Worry Too Much Club" president, I'm going to walk you through just how perfectionism negatively impacts our ability to succeed in life.

It starts with standards. Perfectionists have ridiculously high standards. Some have such have such high standards that they have problems completing work. They sit there slaving away at a project redoing over and over the same small detail. They may find themselves unable to finish a project, simply because it doesn't meet the unrealistic criteria they've established for "perfect." As a result, they get stuck in a vortex of doing and redoing, never being able to make peace with any imperfection. While the world around them progresses and moves onto to the next idea or concept, the perfectionist remains stuck, trapped by their inability to let go of something before it's faultless.

It is a very unsatisfied life that a perfectionist lives; I speak from personal experience. As a recovering fusspot, let me tell you that trying to be perfect is the worst. Nothing is ever good enough. You never feel satisfied. The work you do complete, you can't even celebrate because you're still caught up with the one to two changes you would make, if they would just let you do it over. I lived this life and it was miserable.

Let me tell you a little secret: perfectionism is really about failure. Perfectionists are absolutely and completely terrified of a misstep. Some think people are perfectionists because they want to succeed and change the world and blah-blah-blah. Lies! When you are obsessed with perfection, it's because you are deeply afraid of what might happen if you flounder. Some perfectionists are even so afraid of making a blunder that they just don't even try new things. They avoid activities, hobbies, experiences, and life in general, unless they feel they can be the best in it. They simply cannot enjoy the doing of things, because they are so focused on the fact that may not achieve.

This crippling belief that you shouldn't try unless you can win, and you can't win unless it's perfect doesn't just begin to isolate the perfectionist, it also begins to erode their identities. Imperfection is what makes each of us unique and connected to each other. That means that new ideas or ways of thinking are usually crushed in the emotional cage-match that is a perfectionist's mind. Innovation, creativity, and imagination are all unpredictable, because they don't result in definite outcomes. To a perfectionist, they aren't just problematic, they're the enemy.

Perfectionists also tend to see everything as black-and-white, when the world for the most part is made up of grays. With their all-or-nothing thinking, a perfectionist sees themselves as "good" if people like them, and "bad" if they don't. The worth and value of their life is basically based on an unreliable and ever-changing source of information. Additionally, human relations lead to conflict. This is healthy and helps to challenge and strengthen our own personal beliefs; however, a people-pleasing perfectionist is afraid of any type of dispute, so they avoid challenging conversations out of their fear of upsetting the other person and no longer being perfect in their eyes. As a result, perfectionists endure unhealthy relationships, simply to avoid having to hear they might have a few things to work on.

For a perfectionist, self-worth is completely conditional. "If things go perfectly, if people like me, if my work is well done, then I will be worthy of love." As a result, not only does the individual spend most of their life chasing something that doesn't exist (perfection), but they also avoid hearing feedback out of a fear it might make them seem unworthy (imperfect). Negative feedback is always personal to a perfectionist. "If I failed, if my group failed, if this thing I'm associated with failed, then I'm a failure." This personalizing prevents a perfectionist from getting the feedback needed to evolve and become better. In many ways a perfectionist is doomed to failure because they want so hard to succeed.

PUTTING PEOPLE ON PEDESTALS

In every TV show, movie, and book, there is always one character that everyone else looks up to or fantasizes about being. The cheerleader. The popular girl. The queen of the galaxy. She is the queen of her domain and has all the power. It seems like her life is perfect. However, after living a fairly public life, I no longer look up to these characters.

Instead, I feel for them. A community that expects you to be perfect is a curse worse than death.

As we discussed way back in the chapter on comparison, our brains enjoy putting people on pedestals. "I want to be like her!" Our adoration and intention cast a dewy glow of perfection on the individual. The more we see good in the person, the more their pedestal rises. Eventually they feel like a distant superhuman. On that pedestal we can admire the good qualities we envy, while at the same time we use their faux god-like importance as a reason for why these skills are unattainable for ourselves. We've put them on that pedestal because we want and need to believe that perfection exists, but only for the special people. They become the rare person impervious to error, so that we can find comfort with our own imperfection.

The person you put on a pedestal is put in an unfair position. We have taken away their permission to fail. However, they will inevitably make a mistake. Maybe not today. Maybe not tomorrow. But it will eventually happen. Someday, they will do something stupid. As we already discussed, all humans screw up. However, when they fail in some way—whether big or small—they are not given the same leniency and forgiveness we extend the average, everyday person.

We see this with celebrities all the time. A beloved and adored film actress gets drunk and accidentally tweets something stupid. Suddenly, her years and years of humanitarian work, her breathtaking on-screen performances and her general kindness to strangers don't matter, because one time she said something stupid on the internet. This literally happens once a week. We create pedestals, force our heroes to stand on them, and then get upset and outraged when they do not meet the ideals that a stranger has put on them.

Additionally, putting people on pedestals creates even more pressure for that person to be and always act perfect. If they haven't fallen yet, they become overly aware of what could happen if they do. Every action, response, and moment becomes curated—almost to the point where the real individual gets trapped behind the expectations of others. I cannot even fathom the amount of perfectionist pressure Beyoncé has placed on her every day. Every person I know has her on a pedestal.

HOW TO GET OVER YOUR PERFECTIONIST TENDENCIES

So perfectionism is bad—hopefully we're all on the same page on that one by now. However, if you're like me, a Type A perfectionist, you're probably looking for some black-and-white rules to help you perfectly exist imperfectly. Below are some steps you can take to break up with your need to be perfect.

First and foremost, you're going to need to recognize and self-correct when you are being a judgy witch. It is so easy to fall into the habit of critiquing everything around us for its imperfections. So next time you find yourself judging something or someone, stop yourself and mentally acknowledge the behavior. Then pause and evaluate the value of that critique. Ask yourself questions like, "Can anything actually be improved by pointing this out? Is a person worth less because they don't meet my unrealistic standards of perfection? Am I worth less because I am not perfect?" Forcing yourself to not only face your actions, but also the fear they stem from will help you acknowledge and correct your behavior.

Do one thing each day that scares the bejeebers out of you. Try something you will fail at. Make a decision without planning, indulge in an activity out of your normal schedule, talk to a stranger. Putting ourselves in new scenarios, where "perfect" may not yet be defined helps learn to experience the moment, free of the harsh pressures we usually place on interaction. Take up a light-hearted hobby or an activity you have no previous experience at, one that you know you may not have the skills to do successfully. Pushing ourselves out of our comfort zones and giving ourselves permission to fail in a safe space can translate into us to taking more risks in our day-to-day life.

While you're pushing yourself to work on letting go of control, make sure to make time for you. Lighten your load and turn down extra work. Oftentimes we make ourselves busy to avoid the fact that we are afraid of pushing ourselves and growing. This is one of the little tricks your perfection-loving brain will use to try to keep you from taking risks. Force yourself to say "No" to extra work, so you have the space to grow and make a few mistakes. You are the most important thing in this process, so don't forget that taking time out for *you* isn't selfish or lazy, and doesn't make you a failure. Quite the opposite—it's the ultimate key to your happiness and success.

How to Become Perfectly Imperfect

1. Check Yourself: Acknowledge when you are being hypercritical and examine what those feelings say about you.

2. Take Risks: Try new things and activities that will force you to experience failure on your terms.

3. Make Space to Grow: Ensure you have the time and energy to work on you, by saying no to all that extra work your perfectionist brain says "Yes" to.

CONCLUSION

You've done it—you've reached the end. You've read it all. Congrats! Now what? Remember life is an adventure. True growth and development does not happen overnight. It will be wrought with struggles, battles, and confusion. Remember though that self-doubt can be conquered with gratitude and awareness. Fear can be conquered with thoughtful and strategic focus. Life can be beautiful if you work to see its beauty.

Every chapter in this book boils down to one truth—how you see the world is your choice. Positivity is not about perfection or happiness. Positivity is about hope. It's the belief that tomorrow has the potential to be better than today—no matter how awful today is. Decide today to get to know, appreciate, and love who you are.

Wash away the comparisons to people you will never be and instead unlock the power of knowing your own greatness. Forgive yourself. We all make mistakes and now is the time to focus on how you've grown. You will continue to grow. Accept you are imperfect. We all are imperfect. Life never moves forward when you spend all your time punishing yourself for the past. Focus on the future. Find your community. Be grateful. Be kind. Be fearless. Be you. Find your inner sparkle, and help make the world just a little bit brighter.

ACKNOWLEDGMENTS

I'd like to thank my best friend, Tracie, for putting up with all my crazy phone calls to discuss my ideas, forever being my cheerleader, and making me feel like I belong in this often lonely world. By the same token, I would like to express my gratitude to my dog Data, who never understood why I was stressed out, but always laid by my side to make me feel at ease. I'd also like to acknowledge the bevy of friends who supported me at various stages of this project and believed in me when I was scared to believe in myself.

ANNA O'BRIEN ✧

Anna O'Brien was born with a big mouth, big heart, and big ideas. She shares her life, learning, and fearless fashion sense daily online as Glitter + Lazers. Once a side project, Glitter + Lazers has quickly grown to become a cornerstone in the personal development, fashion, and beauty communities. Anna's work has been featured in major publications across the globe.

Anna has a master's degree from Columbia University where she studied Quantitative Methods in the Social Sciences. Over the past decade she has built a professional career on innovation and creative problem solving. She is best known for her candid and captivating presentation style and her ability to transform difficult concepts into executable steps. Anna lives in NYC with her rescue pup and best friend, Data.

NOTES

1   Richard Lazarus and Susan Folkman. *Stress, Appraisal, and Coping*. New York: Springer, 1984.

2   Sue-Ann Khoo and George D. Bishop. (1997.) "Stress and optimism: Relationships to coping and well-being." *Psychologia: An International Journal of Psychology in the Orient, 40*(1), 29–40. Accessed at: http://onlinelibrary.wiley.com/doi/10.1002/per.2410070407/full

3   Khoo and Bishop, "Stress and optimism."

4   "How to Stop Negative Self-talk." Mayo Clinic. February 18, 2017. https://www.mayoclinic.org/healthy-lifestyle/stress-management/in-depth/positive-thinking/art-20043950.

5   Chad M Burton and Laura A King. "The health benefits of writing about intensely positive experiences." *Science Direct*. Volume 38, Issue 2, April 2004, Pages 150-163. https://www.sciencedirect.com/science/article/pii/S0092656603000588

6   The Power of Positive Thinking." Johns Hopkins Medicine Health Library. Accessed May 2018. https://www.hopkinsmedicine.org/health/healthy_aging/healthy_mind/the-power-of-positive-thinking.

7   Diane Von Ah, Duck-Hee Kang, and Janet S. Carpenter. "Stress, optimism, and social support: Impact on immune responses in breast cancer. January 22, 2007. *Research in Nursing and Health*. Volume 30, Issue 1. http://onlinelibrary.wiley.com/doi/10.1002/nur.20164/full.

8   Glenn Affleck, Howard Tennen, Alex Zautra, Susan Urrows, Micha Abeles, Paul Karoly. "Women's pursuit of personal goals in daily life with fibromyalgia: A value-expectancy analysis." *Journal of Consulting*

and Clinical Psychology, Vol 69(4), Aug 2001, 587–596. https://doi.org/10.1037/0022-006X.69.4.587.

9 Nancy L Costello; Edith E Bragdon; Kathleen C Light; Asgeir Sigurdsson; Shelley Bunting; Karen Grewen; William Maixner. "Temporomandibular disorder and optimism: relationships to ischemic pain sensitivity and interleukin-6." *Journal for the International Association for the Sudy of Pain*. November 2002, Volume 100, Issue 1, p. 99–110. https://doi.org/10.1016/S0304-3959(02)00263-4.

10 H. I. M. Mahler & J. A. Kulik (2000), "Optimism, pessimism and recovery from coronary bypass surgery: Prediction of affect, pain and functional status," *Psychology, Health & Medicine*, 5:4, 347–358, DOI: 10.1080/713690216. https://doi.org/10.1080/713690216.

11 Smith, B.W. & Zautra, A.J. Int. J. Behav. Med. (2004) 11:197. https://doi.org/10.1207/s15327558ijbm1104_2

12 Karen A. Matthews, David C. Glass, Ray H.Rosenman, Rayman W. Bortner. "Competitive drive, pattern a, and coronary heart disease: A further analysis of some data from the Western Collaborative Group Study." Journal of Chronic Diseases. Volume 30, Issue 8, August 1977, Pages 489–498.https://doi.org/10.1016/0021-9681(77)90071-6.

13 How to Stop Negative Self-talk." Mayo Clinic. February 18, 2017. https://www.mayoclinic.org/healthy-lifestyle/stress-management/in-depth/positive-thinking/art-20043950?pg=1.

14 Robyn M. Gill and Jennifer Loh. "The Role of Optimism in Health-Promoting Behaviors in New Primiparous Mothers." *Nursing Research*. September–October 2010, Volume 59, Issue 5, p 348–355.

15 Tara Kraft and Sarah Pressman. "Grin and Bear It: The Influence of Manipulated Positive Facial Expression on the Stress Response." *Psychological Science*, 2012. https://journals.lww.com/nursingresearchonline/Abstract/2010/09000/The_Role_of_Optimism_in_Health_Promoting_Behaviors.5.aspx.

16 Yezen Nwiran and Seph Fontane Pennock. "Resilience in Positive Psychology: Bouncing Back & Going Strong." *Positive Psychology Program: Your One-Stop PP Resource!* March 03, 2017. https://positivepsychologyprogram.com/resilience-in-positive-psychology/.

17 Joe Robinson. "The Resilience of Positivity," *Entrepreneur*. January 2013. http://www.worktolive.info/articles/bid/262631/The-Resilience-of-Positivity.

18 Joe Robinson. "The Link Between Vacations, Productivity, and Work-Life Balance." *Joe Robinson Optimal Performance Strategies*. http://www.worktolive.info/blog/the-link-between-vacations-productivity-and-work-life-balance.

19 Darren Brown, *The Experiments*: "The Secret of Luck." Season 1, Episode 4.

20 Suzanne C. Segerstrom. "Optimism and Resources: Effects on Each Other and on Health over 10 Years." *Egyptian Journal of Medical Human Genetics*. October 19, 2006. https://www.sciencedirect.com/science/article/pii/S0092656606001127.

21 John DeLamater and Daniel Myers. *Social Psychology*. Belmont, CA: Wadsworth Cengage Learning, 2011.

22 Solomon Asch. "Solomon Asch." Viktor E. Frankl, *The Will to Meaning* (1962.) 2000-2007. http://www.panarchy.org/asch/social.pressure.1955.html.

23 "English Dictionary, Thesaurus, & Grammar Help | Oxford Dictionaries." Oxford Dictionaries | English. https://en.oxforddictionaries.com/definition/us/self-awareness.

24 Tasha Eurich. "What Self-Awareness Really Is (and How to Cultivate It.)" *Harvard Business Review*. April 23, 2018. https://hbr.org/2018/01/what-self-awareness-really-is-and-how-to-cultivate-it.

25 Tasha Eurich. *Insight: The Surprising Truth about How Others See Us, How We See Ourselves, and Why the Answers Matter More than We Think.* New York, NY: Currency, 2017.

26 Eurich, *Insight.*

27 Joseph Folkman. "Top Ranked Leaders Know This Secret: Ask For Feedback." *Forbes.* January 08, 2015. https://www.forbes.com/sites/joefolkman/2015/01/08/top-ranked-leaders-know-this-secret-ask-for-feedback/#774294fd3195.

28 John Pencavel. "The Productivity of Working Hours." *The Economic Journal*, 125, no. 589 (April 09, 2014): 2052-076. doi:10.1111/ecoj.12166.

29 Jordan Kisner. "The Politics of Conspicuous Displays of Self-Care." *The New Yorker.* June 19, 2017. https://www.newyorker.com/culture/culture-desk/the-politics-of-selfcare.

30 "Emotions: (Definition and Components of Emotions.)" *Psychology Discussion: Discuss Anything About Psychology.* April 30, 2015. http://www.psychologydiscussion.net/notes/emotions-definition-and-components-of-emotions/666.

31 Jeffrey Walsh. "Three Components of Emotion and the Universal Emotions." Khan Academy. December 15, 2013. https://www.khanacademy.org/science/health-and-medicine/executive-systems-of-the-brain/emotion-lesson/v/three-components-of-emotion-and-the-universal-emotions.

32 Amrisha Vaish, Tobias Grossmann, and Amanda Woodward. "Not All Emotions Are Created Equal: The Negativity Bias in Social-emotional Development." *Advances in Pediatrics.* May 2008. https://www.ncbi.nlm.nih.gov/pmc/articles/PMC3652533/.

33 H. C. Cromwell, R. P. Mears, L. Wan, and N. N. Boutros. "Sensory Gating: A Translational Effort from Basic to Clinical Science." *Advances in Pediatrics.* April 2008. https://www.ncbi.nlm.nih.gov/pubmed/18450171.

34 Sharee N. Light, James A. Coan, Carolyn Zahn-Waxler, Corrina Frye, H. Hill Goldsmith, and Richard J. Davidson. "Empathy Is Associated with Dynamic Change in Prefrontal Brain Electrical Activity during Positive Emotion in Children." *Advances in Pediatrics*. 2009. https://www.ncbi. nlm.nih.gov/pmc/articles/PMC2717040/.

35 Fabian Gander, René T. Proyer, Willibald Ruch, and Tobias Wyss. "Strength-Based Positive Interventions: Further Evidence for Their Potential in Enhancing Well-Being and Alleviating Depression." *Journal of Happiness Studies*, 14, no. 4 (2012): 1241-259. doi:10.1007/s10902-012-9380-0.

36 Christina CongletonBritta K. HölzelSara W. Lazar, and *Harvard Business Review*. "Mindfulness Can Literally Change Your Brain." *Harvard Business Review*. March 12, 2018. https://hbr.org/2015/01/mindfulness-can-literally-change-your-brain.

37 Neff, Kristin D., Stephanie S. Rude, and Kristin L. Kirkpatrick. "An Examination of Self-compassion in Relation to Positive Psychological Functioning and Personality Traits." *Egyptian Journal of Medical Human Genetics*. October 02, 2006. https://www.sciencedirect.com/science/article/pii/S009265660600095X.

38 Erin Reiny. "Why We Don't Use the Word "Bully" to Label Kids." StopBullying.gov. October 23, 2013. https://www.stopbullying.gov/blog/2013/10/23/why-we-don't-use-word-"bully"-label-kids.

39 Christina Salmivalli. "Bullying and the Peer Group: A Review." *Aggression and Violent Behavior*, 15, no. 2 (2010): 112-20. doi:10.1016/j. avb.2009.08.007.

40 "Anti-Bullying Charity." Ditch the Label. http://ditchthelabel.org/.

41 Miranda Smith. "IThe Effects of Exercise on the Brain and How It Could Shape Future Medicine and Change the Way GPs Treat Their Patients." Medlink Conference, March 2013. https://medlink-uk.net/wp-content/uploads/pathology-projects-2013/SmithM.pdf.

42 Helen Street. "Exploring Relationships between Goal Setting, Goal
    Pursuit and Depression: A Review." Taylor & Francis. August 22, 2006.
    https://www.tandfonline.com/doi/abs/10.1080/00050060210001706736.

43 Jeremy Dean. *Making Habits, Breaking Habits: Why We Do Things, Why
    We Dont, and How to Make Any Change Stick.* New York: Bristol Parks
    Books, 2016.

44 Note that you should never feel like you have to change your body or
    size to fit in or be accepted.

45 Edwin A. Locke, Karyll N. Shaw, Lise M. Saari, and Gary P. Latham.
    "Goal Setting and Task Performance." *American Psychological
    Association.* 1981. http://psycnet.apa.org/journals/bul/90/1/125/.

46 Statistic Brain. "New Years Resolution Statistics." *Statistic Brain
    Research Institute.* January 9, 2018. https://www.statisticbrain.com/
    new-years-resolution-statistics/.

47 Jane E. Brody. "The Surprising Effects of Loneliness on Health."
    The New York Times. December 11, 2017. https://www.nytimes.
    com/2017/12/11/well/mind/how-loneliness-affects-our-health.html.

48 Carla M. Perissinotto, Irena Stijacic Cenzer, and Kenneth E. Covinsky.
    "Loneliness in Older Persons: A Predictor of Functional Decline and
    Death." National Center for Biotechnology Information. July 23, 2012.
    https://www.ncbi.nlm.nih.gov/pmc/articles/PMC4383762/.

49 Raheel Mushtaq, Sheikh Shoib, Tabindah Shah, and Sahil Mushtaq.
    "Relationship Between Loneliness, Psychiatric Disorders and Physical
    Health? A Review on the Psychological Aspects of Loneliness." National
    Center for Biotechnology Information. September 2014. https://www.
    ncbi.nlm.nih.gov/pmc/articles/PMC4225959/.

50 Sarvada Chandra Tiwari. "Loneliness: A Disease?" National Center for
    Biotechnology Information. December 2013. https://www.ncbi.nlm.nih.
    gov/pmc/articles/PMC3890922/.

51 Mushtag, "Relationship Between Loneliness, Psychiatric Disorders and Physical Health."

52 Alexandra Sifferlin. "Why Your Cold Feels Worse When You're Lonely." *Time*. March 30, 2017. http://time.com/4715823/cold-symptoms-sick-loneliness/.

53 Natalie Shoemaker. "Study Links Social Isolation to Heart Risks." *Big Think*. January 26, 2015. http://bigthink.com/ideafeed/study-links-social-isolation-to-heart-risks.

54 Natalie Shoemaker. "Study Links Social Isolation to Heart Risks." *Big Think*. January 26, 2015. http://bigthink.com/ideafeed/study-links-social-isolation-to-heart-risks.

55 James House, K. Landis, and D. Umberson. "Social Relationships and Health." Science 241, no. 4865 (1988): 540-45. doi:10.1126/science.3399889.

56 Richard Lang. "Richard Lang, MD, MPH." Cleveland Clinic. https://my.clevelandclinic.org/staff_directory/staff_display?doctorid=733.

57 "You Don't Have To Be Alone – Here Are 5 Ways To Beat Loneliness." *Best Health Magazine* Canada. May 10, 2018. http://www.besthealthmag.ca/best-you/mental-health/beat-loneliness/.

58 Samantha Marshall. "Ankles Away: Cosmetic Surgery for Cankles." *Marie Claire*. October 11, 2017. https://www.marieclaire.com/beauty/a6541/cankle-surgery-trend/.

59 Alan Fogel. "What Is Body Sense?" *Psychology Today*. July 21, 2009. https://www.psychologytoday.com/us/blog/body-sense/200907/what-is-body-sense.

60 Channing Sargent. "7 Weird Things That Happen to Your Body When You Cry." HelloGiggles. February 17, 2017. https://hellogiggles.com/lifestyle/health-fitness/7-weird-things-that-happen-to-your-body-when-you-cry/.

61 Judith Orloff M.D. "The Healing Power of Tears." Judith Orloff MD. March 29, 2018. https://drjudithorloff.com/the-healing-power-of-tears/.

62 Hart, M.D., Patricia. "What Is the Mind-Body Connection?" Taking Charge of Your Health & Wellbeing. https://www.takingcharge.csh.umn.edu/what-is-the-mind-body-connection.

63 Mandy Oaklander. "This Quick Body Scan Meditation Helps You Go To Sleep." *Time*. April 28, 2017. http://time.com/4737068/body-scan-meditation-sleep/.

64 Alina Tugend. "The Satisfaction, and Annoyance, of Complaining." *The New York Times*. May 03, 2013. https://www.nytimes.com/2013/05/04/your-money/the-satisfaction-and-annoyance-of-complaining.html.

65 Mark D. Alicke, and James C. Braun. "Complaining Behavior in Social Interaction." Philosophy of the Social Sciences. June 1, 1992. http://journals.sagepub.com/doi/10.1177/0146167292183004.

66 Stephanie Vozza. "Why Complaining May Be Dangerous To Your Health." *Fast Company*. January 12, 2015. https://www.fastcompany.com/3040672/why-complaining-may-be-dangerous-to-your-health.

67 Sarah Mae Sincero. "Three Different Kinds of Stress – Acute, Episodic and Chronic." Observation Bias. September 10, 2012. https://explorable.com/three-different-kinds-of-stress.

68 I made these numbers up.

69 Fariss Samarrai. "Human Brains Are Hardwired for Empathy, Friendship, Study Shows." *UVA Today*. August 21, 2013. https://news.virginia.edu/content/human-brains-are-hardwired-empathy-friendship-study-shows.

70 Susan S. Lang. "Americans' Circle of Confidantes Has Shrunk to Two People | Cornell Chronicle." Genetic Switches Play Big Role in Human Evolution. November 1, 2011. http://news.cornell.edu/stories/2011/11/americans-circle-confidantes-has-shrunk-two-people.

71 Abdullah Almaatouq, Laura Radaelli, Alex Pentland, and Erez Shmueli. "Are You Your Friends' Friend? Poor Perception of Friendship Ties Limits the Ability to Promote Behavioral Change." PLOS Medicine. March 22, 2016. http://journals.plos.org/plosone/article?id=10.1371/journal.pone.0151588.

72 "Maslow's Hierarchy of Needs." Wikipedia. July 15, 2018. https://en.wikipedia.org/wiki/Maslow's_hierarchy_of_needs.

73 "The Health Benefits of Good Friends." Mayo Clinic. September 28, 2016. https://www.mayoclinic.org/healthy-lifestyle/adult-health/in-depth/friendships/art-20044860.

74 "About." Tanja Hollander. https://www.tanjahollander.com/about/.

75 "Alaska Suicide Follow-Back Study: Final Report." *PsycEXTRA Dataset*, 2007. doi:10.1037/e431442008-001.

76 Ken Gobbo and Solvegi Shmulsky. "Helping Students Manage Perfectionism and Procrastination." College Teaching 47, no. 4 (1999): 148. doi:10.1080/87567559909595806

77 Gobbo, "Helping Students Manage Perfectionism and Procrastination."